First Published in 2016
By Live Canon Ltd
www.livecanon.co.uk

All rights reserved

© Live Canon 2016

978-1-909703-18-6

Edited by Helen Eastman
for Live Canon

154 POEMS BY 154 CONTEMPORARY POETS, IN RESPONSE TO SHAKESPEARE'S 154 SONNETS

Contents

I

From fairest creatures we desire increase,
That thereby beauty's rose might never die,
But as the riper should by time decease,
His tender heir might bear his memory:
But thou contracted to thine own bright eyes,
Feed'st thy light's flame with self-substantial fuel,
Making a famine where abundance lies,
Thy self thy foe, to thy sweet self too cruel:
Thou that art now the world's fresh ornament,
And only herald to the gaudy spring,
Within thine own bud buriest thy content,
And tender churl mak'st waste in niggarding:
  Pity the world, or else this glutton be,
  To eat the world's due, by the grave and thee.

Beauty must repeat
Mark A. Hill

Each one of us breathes a life
created in a moment of beauty,
mute *The Larkin,* and
in my wordy issue seek solution
procreation is increase not dilution.

Invest yourself,
make husband of your seed,
do not bring famine where food is plenty,
fill the vase of life with bloom
leave your lover never empty.

Do not pause a moment to consider
the boys' pre-conceptions, the other lovers,
never stall the finishing
accept all the bug eye offers.

Finger hard on the soft pork belly
of what is out there; living means
pawing dampness tenderly
meeting loving ends.

Feed on what could be struck or strikes you
what you swipe, not with AMEX, but with your i.d,
your trace, your content
which will be stowed away in your peerless progeny.

II

When forty winters shall besiege thy brow,
And dig deep trenches in thy beauty's field,
Thy youth's proud livery so gazed on now,
Will be a tatter'd weed of small worth held:
Then being asked, where all thy beauty lies,
Where all the treasure of thy lusty days;
To say, within thine own deep sunken eyes,
Were an all-eating shame, and thriftless praise.
How much more praise deserv'd thy beauty's use,
If thou couldst answer 'This fair child of mine
Shall sum my count, and make my old excuse,'
Proving his beauty by succession thine!
  This were to be new made when thou art old,
  And see thy blood warm when thou feel'st it cold.

Son
Antony Dunn

At five, you find your way into our bed
with all your small, smooth body and great heat
and find your restless, forty-something dad
besieged by dreams – the one in which I cheat,
the one in which I marvellously rage,
the dreadful dream in which I love someone
I've never met or someone half my age,
the one in which I leave us all undone.
I'm sorry for this pile of selves, my son –
this uninvited, tattered crowd – but you
should know, somewhere among them, there is one
whose dreams are still, still, beautiful and true.
Alone among these forty-something men,
how must you know, son, which will wake, and when?

III

Look in thy glass and tell the face thou viewest
Now is the time that face should form another;
Whose fresh repair if now thou not renewest,
Thou dost beguile the world, unbless some mother.
For where is she so fair whose unear'd womb
Disdains the tillage of thy husbandry?
Or who is he so fond will be the tomb,
Of his self-love to stop posterity?
Thou art thy mother's glass and she in thee
Calls back the lovely April of her prime;
So thou through windows of thine age shalt see,
Despite of wrinkles this thy golden time.
  But if thou live, remember'd not to be,
  Die single and thine image dies with thee.

Immortality
Doreen Hinchliffe

Don't let the mirror fool you. Now is not
the time for breeding. It's a vain ambition
to hope your kids preserve your image. What
they'll look like's far from certain. The transmission
of your genes won't guarantee survival
of your face, or even your ideals -
each tot will turn into a teenage rival
and grind all your beliefs beneath its heels.
Progeny can't be trusted. They'll only twist
and falsify your truth. Better by far
to dedicate yourself to writing, resist
convention, let poetry speak of who you are.
Die childless. Leave black ink when you are gone.
Then, white as snow, your essence will live on.

IV

Unthrifty loveliness, why dost thou spend
Upon thy self thy beauty's legacy?
Nature's bequest gives nothing, but doth lend,
And being frank she lends to those are free:
Then, beauteous niggard, why dost thou abuse
The bounteous largess given thee to give?
Profitless usurer, why dost thou use
So great a sum of sums, yet canst not live?
For having traffic with thy self alone,
Thou of thy self thy sweet self dost deceive:
Then how when nature calls thee to be gone,
What acceptable audit canst thou leave?
  Thy unused beauty must be tombed with thee,
  Which, used, lives th' executor to be.

IV
Michael Kelleher

Beauty imagined as a kind of currency within an economic system run by Nature. Nature lends this currency in the short term at high rates. Once the term is up the currency loses all value and is returned to the bank. Those who ignore these facts and choose not to profit by means of procreation do so at their peril. Better to imagine the loan as a kind of deadline and to try to profit at a higher rate of return than the interest Nature charges. When the term is up, an accounting will be required. At such time the borrower must return the amount of the original loan plus interest. Unbalanced accounts will result in a sentence of death to the borrower. Beauty will go to the grave, where, unseen, its currency has no value.

V

Those hours, that with gentle work did frame
The lovely gaze where every eye doth dwell,
Will play the tyrants to the very same
And that unfair which fairly doth excel;
For never-resting time leads summer on
To hideous winter, and confounds him there;
Sap checked with frost, and lusty leaves quite gone,
Beauty o'er-snowed and bareness every where:
Then were not summer's distillation left,
A liquid prisoner pent in walls of glass,
Beauty's effect with beauty were bereft,
Nor it, nor no remembrance what it was:
  But flowers distill'd, though they with winter meet,
  Leese but their show; their substance still lives sweet.

Alder
Seán Hewitt

Walking by the lake at dusk, I stop by an alder.
He is quiet, lonely I think, sits by the water with an air
of conspiracy. He greets me by lowering a branch

across my path, and I notice a twig hanging from it
by a thread, like a string-puppet. It is twisting in the wind,
dreaming of spinning itself loose. I look up at the tree:

Do you mean, I ask, *that time moves in circles?*
That it is a spiral, a repetition? Slowly, he shakes
his head and returns, disappointed, to silence.

Beside me, a coot pushes off from the reedbed -
I watch her shear a clean line through the water.
The alder creaks and begins to spin the twig again,

moving his fingers up and down and watching
the little body dance. *Is it that we are sewn to time?*
That it holds us together? He stops. I remember how

one night, you thought of spinning your life on a rope,
getting free of it, then held back. I think, *what a perfect*
tether can link us still to time. The alder watches gently

as I start to cry, then lifts his arm. I thank him, head bent,
and walk on. In the lake, a moorhen dives and resurfaces,
unpicking a seam. The water unravels behind her.

VI

Then let not winter's ragged hand deface,
In thee thy summer, ere thou be distill'd:
Make sweet some vial; treasure thou some place
With beauty's treasure ere it be self-kill'd.
That use is not forbidden usury,
Which happies those that pay the willing loan;
That's for thy self to breed another thee,
Or ten times happier, be it ten for one;
Ten times thy self were happier than thou art,
If ten of thine ten times refigur'd thee:
Then what could death do if thou shouldst depart,
Leaving thee living in posterity?
  Be not self-will'd, for thou art much too fair
  To be death's conquest and make worms thine heir.

Posterity
Lorraine Mariner

Winter's ragged hand takes mine
and I cough from December
through to March.

We mark your birthday
watching a film starring
the scantily clad child

of actors we once desired,
before their divorce,
the botched facial work.

Crack open the Lemsip,
dust down that video tape,
refigure them.

VII

Lo! in the orient when the gracious light
Lifts up his burning head, each under eye
Doth homage to his new-appearing sight,
Serving with looks his sacred majesty;
And having climb'd the steep-up heavenly hill,
Resembling strong youth in his middle age,
Yet mortal looks adore his beauty still,
Attending on his golden pilgrimage:
But when from highmost pitch, with weary car,
Like feeble age, he reeleth from the day,
The eyes, 'fore duteous, now converted are
From his low tract, and look another way:
  So thou, thyself outgoing in thy noon:
  Unlook'd, on diest unless thou get a son.

Eclipsed
NJ Hynes

The dogs howl and household gods shiver
as the sun is dimmed and living colour dies,
a world reduced to black and white – but tides
continue to rise. The moon draws to her
growing seas and awkward monthly pains;
her milky light is gone, yet she covers
the golden sun, casts a shadow over
its flame. Her gravity and mass remain
even when her features disappear;
a stoic lid to the star's burning light.
Unlike the sun, she will always stay near,
whether full or perilously slight.
Now be glad, dear woman, expectant one,
for a moon-faced daughter – not a son.

VIII

Music to hear, why hear'st thou music sadly?
Sweets with sweets war not, joy delights in joy:
Why lov'st thou that which thou receiv'st not gladly,
Or else receiv'st with pleasure thine annoy?
If the true concord of well-tuned sounds,
By unions married, do offend thine ear,
They do but sweetly chide thee, who confounds
In singleness the parts that thou shouldst bear.
Mark how one string, sweet husband to another,
Strikes each in each by mutual ordering;
Resembling sire and child and happy mother,
Who, all in one, one pleasing note do sing:
  Whose speechless song being many, seeming one,
  Sings this to thee: 'Thou single wilt prove none.'

Counterpoint
Miriam Nash

There's that music, just beyond my ear,
sweet to imagine, sweeter to ignore:
it draws our unborn children from the air,
listen—their songs already hum our score.
We'll buy them instruments, we'll scrape a band,
you on your old drum-kit, me on bass—
they'll take the melody. Unplugged, unplanned,
we'll improvise a syncopated grace.
Is this song mine? I strike the single note
that jars the orchestra, and weigh its tone:
a woman who loves music may devote
full voice to compositions of her own.
My love, whatever riffs our lives create—
let's revel in the counterpoint, and wait.

IX

Is it for fear to wet a widow's eye,
That thou consum'st thy self in single life?
Ah! if thou issueless shalt hap to die,
The world will wail thee like a makeless wife;
The world will be thy widow and still weep
That thou no form of thee hast left behind,
When every private widow well may keep
By children's eyes, her husband's shape in mind:
Look! what an unthrift in the world doth spend
Shifts but his place, for still the world enjoys it;
But beauty's waste hath in the world an end,
And kept unused the user so destroys it.
  No love toward others in that bosom sits
  That on himself such murd'rous shame commits.

Issue
Mel Pryor

Troubled much of the time
she attempts to suppress her troubles

by spending her time making things.
She bakes cupcakes and almond loaf

and makes collages for the front of cards
she sends to her and to his relatives

on their birthdays, and she makes jackets
for the babies in Syria

usually in yellow wool though
sometimes in blue or candy pink.

Whenever she folds a jacket up,
places it in the plastic bag for the charity,

she feels the breath pressed out of it,
hears the clickclicking

of the little irregular tender heartbeat
knitted into its centre

disappear into thin air.
His voice is like the needle

on a sewing machine. He says
he's not ready, they're not ready

for the children thing. She knits booties
to match the jackets, small vests, small

leggings with elasticated waists,
bonnets, and mittens, all-in-ones.

X

For shame! deny that thou bear'st love to any,
Who for thy self art so unprovident.
Grant, if thou wilt, thou art belov'd of many,
But that thou none lov'st is most evident:
For thou art so possess'd with murderous hate,
That 'gainst thy self thou stick'st not to conspire,
Seeking that beauteous roof to ruinate
Which to repair should be thy chief desire.
O! change thy thought, that I may change my mind:
Shall hate be fairer lodg'd than gentle love?
Be, as thy presence is, gracious and kind,
Or to thyself at least kind-hearted prove:
  Make thee another self for love of me,
  That beauty still may live in thine or thee.

South Stair Bow Window
Becky Cullen

They roll out the glinting tapestry
and shake; it sings into place, shrugs
its sharpness into the arched stone bay.
A sheet of diamonds, carnelian-edged,
squares of berry and caged jay
scored and ground and bound in bronze.
It is geometry –
rotates like semaphore, or clocks.

We've been circling since the first buds,
pass on the staircase, beneath the panes
of cooled molten quartz, dress
while outside a feather catches
on a casement snick. Tension holds
the glass in place. Inside, it's moving.

XI

As fast as thou shalt wane, so fast thou grow'st
In one of thine, from that which thou departest;
And that fresh blood which youngly thou bestow'st,
Thou mayst call thine when thou from youth convertest,
Herein lives wisdom, beauty, and increase;
Without this folly, age, and cold decay:
If all were minded so, the times should cease
And threescore year would make the world away.
Let those whom nature hath not made for store,
Harsh, featureless, and rude, barrenly perish:
Look, whom she best endow'd, she gave thee more;
Which bounteous gift thou shouldst in bounty cherish:
  She carv'd thee for her seal, and meant thereby,
  Thou shouldst print more, not let that copy die.

Censer

Ali Lewis

"from that which thou departest"

A boy walking to the swings, his cider huge,
big as his chest, and the plastic so thin
any squeeze will blub the sticky warmth
over his hands, onto his jeans, and then
what would his risk have been? He rolls
a spliff, his fingers thick, unpractised,
cold, the paper flimsy, underweight —
but what he tongues will part her lips -
the girl he meets - and the cider he has won.
It feels good to watch her drink, to wipe
the drips from her chin. He sits. She sits.
They smoke and shuttle cider till its sour,
till he stands and leans his weight into her,
pushes, and the girl exhales — and swings.

XII

When I do count the clock that tells the time,
And see the brave day sunk in hideous night;
When I behold the violet past prime,
And sable curls, all silvered o'er with white;
When lofty trees I see barren of leaves,
Which erst from heat did canopy the herd,
And summer's green all girded up in sheaves,
Borne on the bier with white and bristly beard,
Then of thy beauty do I question make,
That thou among the wastes of time must go,
Since sweets and beauties do themselves forsake
And die as fast as they see others grow;
  And nothing 'gainst Time's scythe can make defence
  Save breed, to brave him when he takes thee hence.

Young Couples by the Hotel Pool, Sierra Bernia
Christopher North

Sun blazes its way towards the pine-tree ridge,
Late after-noon now offering hints of evening,
The day moon just beginning to gleam,
Their light conversation small coda

To the shouts, splashes and laughter before.
One smiles down at his girlfriend, waving a hand,
The other lies flat, arms raised beseeching the sky
As the fourth, a golden girl, murmurs in sun worship.

They are the beautiful people, childless, monied —
Their cars glint in the parking – shades of the hotel.
They are moving toward pre-prandial aperitifs
And endless, gilt edged years of themselves.

Tomorrow they leave for the city, will greet their dogs,
Their children, who welcome them with wagging tails.

XIII

O! that you were your self; but, love you are
No longer yours, than you your self here live:
Against this coming end you should prepare,
And your sweet semblance to some other give:
So should that beauty which you hold in lease
Find no determination; then you were
Yourself again, after yourself's decease,
When your sweet issue your sweet form should bear.
Who lets so fair a house fall to decay,
Which husbandry in honour might uphold,
Against the stormy gusts of winter's day
And barren rage of death's eternal cold?
  O! none but unthrifts. Dear my love, you know,
  You had a father: let your son say so.

Yourself again
Andrew Rudd

Soon as you've gone, they rummage through your stuff.
The body's hardly cold before they start
the long post-mortem, digging for your heart,
dissecting poems, twisting words. Enough.

You wanted your lover's beauty to survive
in his children, to keep his perfect face
familiar in this distant, future place.
It sort-of worked, these poems are still alive

and in them you're still visible. In verse
you got your wish. Your face, his face, these lines;
a sonnet your sweet form, those lasting rhymes
his look. Though wintertime has done its worst

your DNA, your lineaments endure.
O that you were yourself? But love, you are.

XIV

Not from the stars do I my judgement pluck;
And yet methinks I have astronomy,
But not to tell of good or evil luck,
Of plagues, of dearths, or seasons' quality;
Nor can I fortune to brief minutes tell,
Pointing to each his thunder, rain and wind,
Or say with princes if it shall go well
By oft predict that I in heaven find:
But from thine eyes my knowledge I derive,
And constant stars in them I read such art
As 'Truth and beauty shall together thrive,
If from thyself, to store thou wouldst convert';
  Or else of thee this I prognosticate:
  'Thy end is truth's and beauty's doom and date.'

Aquarius
Miranda Peake

All day we lived with the thought of you,
celeriac remoulade and Boeuf Bourguignon
covered our plates as we lifted two glasses
of sun and toasted your name. Later
we wandered down Tottenham Court Road,
stopping for love seats and dining room chairs.
We sat on sofas and questioned the depth
of shelves. We measured rugs with our feet
and imagined them here and there. We mustn't
get carried away, I said, revolving slowly
around an occasional table. In Heal's café
we turned retrograde, talking about the house
again, the rooms downstairs, how they take the sun,
their double aspect smiles. The Japanese print
and the Lalique bowl, frosty like a moon,
whether to keep it or whether to sell it, and what
of all this beauty, if you're not here to live in it.

XV

When I consider every thing that grows
Holds in perfection but a little moment,
That this huge stage presenteth nought but shows
Whereon the stars in secret influence comment;
When I perceive that men as plants increase,
Cheered and checked even by the self-same sky,
Vaunt in their youthful sap, at height decrease,
And wear their brave state out of memory;
Then the conceit of this inconstant stay
Sets you most rich in youth before my sight,
Where wasteful Time debateth with decay
To change your day of youth to sullied night,
  And all in war with Time for love of you,
  As he takes from you, I engraft you new.

Musée de You

Andrew George

No single work of art, even a sonnet
can capture and transmit your gorgeous essence
to the future's doubtful hordes. Far from it.
Museums are required to keep you present.
A history wing devoted to your forebears,
sepia-smart in earnest village centres,
with maps to show their slow migrations, or there's
a gallery with statues of your parents,
where themed displays are canvassing the walls
with brownie badges, legwarmers and bobs,
a slender glove you wore to Freshers' Ball,
a rubber pair retrieved from your first job,
one finger lost and flecked with bloody spatters.
It's all here. Because it all matters.

XVI

But wherefore do not you a mightier way
Make war upon this bloody tyrant, Time?
And fortify your self in your decay
With means more blessed than my barren rhyme?
Now stand you on the top of happy hours,
And many maiden gardens, yet unset,
With virtuous wish would bear you living flowers,
Much liker than your painted counterfeit:
So should the lines of life that life repair,
Which this, Time's pencil, or my pupil pen,
Neither in inward worth nor outward fair,
Can make you live your self in eyes of men.
  To give away yourself, keeps yourself still,
    And you must live, drawn by your own sweet skill.

Sixteen
Maeve Henry

But as I ease clean boxers in your drawer
my hand knocks up against a pack of three.
I sit down, winded, on your tousled bed
where school books jostle with art magazines,
and scan the door frame's rule of pencil marks
which measure out our growing loss of you.
Each birthday's been a little death, a kiss
goodbye. The character we knew has smudged
with each year's fresh re-inking; look how fast
you have become yourself, not me, not him.
With what strange pain and pride, my quiet son,
I picture you, cocksure among the girls,
and years from now, see standing in their place
a woman whose sweet skill draws your son's face.

XVII

Who will believe my verse in time to come,
If it were fill'd with your most high deserts?
Though yet heaven knows it is but as a tomb
Which hides your life, and shows not half your parts.
If I could write the beauty of your eyes,
And in fresh numbers number all your graces,
The age to come would say 'This poet lies;
Such heavenly touches ne'er touch'd earthly faces.'
So should my papers, yellow'd with their age,
Be scorn'd, like old men of less truth than tongue,
And your true rights be term'd a poet's rage
And stretched metre of an antique song:
  But were some child of yours alive that time,
  You should live twice, – in it, and in my rhyme.

17
Tim Richardson

If I recall you as you were that day
(Our sad reversals posted back in time):
The cracking elms falling in the March haze
While the monarchy of my distrait rhymes
Suffered a deposition so abject
That I took to tracing the arc of your eyes
In each face I saw after, without respect
For time, grace or colour – since all was denied.
Still I see you, though now in different form
For those large beginnings are shrunk to a stall
Shelt'ring memories that keep me falsely warm:
Kindling for dreams smothered under a pall.
If I had not loved you that cold dark spring
Could I have known the joy these wounds would bring?

XVIII

Shall I compare thee to a summer's day?
Thou art more lovely and more temperate:
Rough winds do shake the darling buds of May,
And summer's lease hath all too short a date:
Sometime too hot the eye of heaven shines,
And often is his gold complexion dimm'd,
And every fair from fair sometime declines,
By chance, or nature's changing course untrimm'd:
But thy eternal summer shall not fade,
Nor lose possession of that fair thou ow'st,
Nor shall death brag thou wander'st in his shade,
When in eternal lines to time thou grow'st,
  So long as men can breathe, or eyes can see,
  So long lives this, and this gives life to thee.

Shakespeare in Space
Abigail Parry

Shall I compare thee to the Milky Way?
Thou art more restless and disorderly.
A raging ball of gas at least obeys
The laws of thermal flux and entropy.

Tornados tear across the face of Mars,
The lava pits of Venus roil and shriek,
The Sun erupts in white-hot solar flares,
But you – you make a nebula look meek.

Black holes and supernovas tend to sit
In orbits more or less predictable.
But Newton could not brag that you submit
To one scintilla of his Principles.

But ah, my little quark, so charmed and strange,
There's not one atom of you I would change.

Devouring Time, blunt thou the lion's paws,
And make the earth devour her own sweet brood;
Pluck the keen teeth from the fierce tiger's jaws,
And burn the long-liv'd phoenix, in her blood;
Make glad and sorry seasons as thou fleets,
And do whate'er thou wilt, swift-footed Time,
To the wide world and all her fading sweets;
But I forbid thee one most heinous crime:
O! carve not with thy hours my love's fair brow,
Nor draw no lines there with thine antique pen;
Him in thy course untainted do allow
For beauty's pattern to succeeding men.
  Yet, do thy worst old Time: despite thy wrong,
  My love shall in my verse ever live young.

Locked in the lines
Peter Kenny

Devouring Time, blunt thou the lion's paws,
    NO. LET THE CLAWS TEAR THROUGH ME
And make the earth devour her own sweet brood;
    INTER ME IN CLOYING CLAY.
Pluck the keen teeth from the fierce tiger's jaws,
    I'M CENTURIES IMPRISONED
And burn the long-lived phoenix in her blood;
    INSIDE THIS 14 BARRED CAGE.
Make glad and sorry seasons as thou fleet'st,
    PEERING OUT FROM THUMBED PAGES
And do whate'er thou wilt, swift-footed Time,
    I WATCH YOUR DAMSELFLY LIVES,
To the wide world and all her fading sweets;
    CLEVER CHILDREN WIZENING
But I forbid thee one most heinous crime:
    INTO CRONES AND BROKEN MEN.
O, carve not with thy hours my love's fair brow,
    MY LIFE WAS MINE, NOT HIS.
Nor draw no lines there with thine antique pen;
    BLACK TONGUED, I WOULD DRINK INK
Him in thy course untainted do allow
    TILL I DRAINED THE LAKE OF TIME.
For beauty's pattern to succeeding men.
    CAN YOU SEE ME TRAPPED IN RAGE?
Yet, do thy worst, old Time: despite thy wrong,
    EVER DO I HAUNT THIS PAGE.
My love shall in my verse ever live young.

XX

A woman's face with nature's own hand painted,
Hast thou, the master mistress of my passion;
A woman's gentle heart, but not acquainted
With shifting change, as is false women's fashion:
An eye more bright than theirs, less false in rolling,
Gilding the object whereupon it gazeth;
A man in hue all 'hues' in his controlling,
Which steals men's eyes and women's souls amazeth.
And for a woman wert thou first created;
Till Nature, as she wrought thee, fell a-doting,
And by addition me of thee defeated,
By adding one thing to my purpose nothing.
  But since she prick'd thee out for women's pleasure,
  Mine be thy love and thy love's use their treasure.

Ladyboy
Konstandinos Mahoney

A woman's face and form, bar one small detail,
Smooth-legged she strides along the Silom Soi,
Allure and pulling power never failing,
My Bangkok belle, my beau, my ladyboy.
Her painted face can trick the reeling sailor,
catch husband tourist poet unaware,
together stagger from the Pat Pong parlour,
and through the back door mount the groaning stairs.
She lip synchs Whitney at the Colosseum,
the songs she sings to me are out of tune,
but being so, are sweet, so carpe-diem,
in nature's off key love notes let us croon.
With ying and yang together for good measure,
The him in her and her in him my treasure.

XXI

So is it not with me as with that Muse,
Stirr'd by a painted beauty to his verse,
Who heaven itself for ornament doth use
And every fair with his fair doth rehearse,
Making a couplement of proud compare'
With sun and moon, with earth and sea's rich gems,
With April's first-born flowers, and all things rare,
That heaven's air in this huge rondure hems.
O! let me, true in love, but truly write,
And then believe me, my love is as fair
As any mother's child, though not so bright
As those gold candles fix'd in heaven's air:
  Let them say more that like of hearsay well;
  I will not praise that purpose not to sell.

The Rival
Jon Stone

The rival, when he dresses, dresses
in hideous kisses.
Upgraded, unupbraided, he convalesces
with his critic-accomplices,

who, far from concurring that less is
more, continue to ransack the last of the dream-palaces
for analogies with which to bless his
latest work of blistering blisses:

berubied boiseried linen-presses,
bediamonded friezes and cornices,
bemoonstoned princesses,
bemoonstoned princesses' clitorises.

The chamber fills, the air thickens with trinketry.
The cinema sinks into a tinctured sea
while the rival oh so gently effervesces.

XXII

My glass shall not persuade me I am old,
So long as youth and thou are of one date;
But when in thee time's furrows I behold,
Then look I death my days should expiate.
For all that beauty that doth cover thee,
Is but the seemly raiment of my heart,
Which in thy breast doth live, as thine in me:
How can I then be elder than thou art?
O! therefore love, be of thyself so wary
As I, not for myself, but for thee will;
Bearing thy heart, which I will keep so chary
As tender nurse her babe from faring ill.
  Presume not on thy heart when mine is slain,
  Thou gav'st me thine not to give back again.

Give me your unsteady knife, doc. Give me your hand, friend
('Medicine' by Raymond Carver)
Rosie Shepperd

This is the 2nd opinion I did not get and not because it is too late.
It is not the opinion I do not know. It is the one I did not get.

This news is not new or news to you any more than it is to me.
It is a shadow on the wall of Plato's cave we name but do not see.

It is not the distance that echoes within the chambers of my heart.
It is the space between the words I say that hears what is unheard.

You do not have to say yes to this; this is the thing we did not expect.
I cannot say no to this; this choice is a choice but it's not the one I get.

The care you want to give to me is the care I'd planned to give to you.
The dark that lies behind your eyes, it will lie to you but not to me.

My love, you'll find this quite by chance when you need it to be found.
My love, you are right I am thankful and I need to write this down.

I am the unsteady hand, doctor. Steady your left hand, my friend.
You're not a hand to steady a knife; I am the knife. Steady, my hand.

XXIII

As an unperfect actor on the stage,
Who with his fear is put beside his part,
Or some fierce thing replete with too much rage,
Whose strength's abundance weakens his own heart;
So I, for fear of trust, forget to say
The perfect ceremony of love's rite,
And in mine own love's strength seem to decay,
O'ercharg'd with burthen of mine own love's might.
O! let my looks be then the eloquence
And dumb presagers of my speaking breast,
Who plead for love, and look for recompense,
More than that tongue that more hath more express'd.
　O! learn to read what silent love hath writ:
　To hear with eyes belongs to love's fine wit.

Miscast Actors
Marcus Smith

You're star-like in the comic mask you wear,
But in the dark demur, 'Passion steps on me'
As quickly as you lay your body bare,
And we're living a tragic French movie.
Afterwards, you run from the promise I give,
Laugh off any praise like a miscast actor
Blaming the script for work that doesn't live
In the spotlight of a demanding director.
Let's not play *I'm-not-as-good-as-you-think*.
Neither am I. If I can't love you as you are
Behind the masks, I might as well lip-synch
'How Does Anyone Reach A Distant Star?'
Please don't shove us into a comedy.
I don't want to love you in a tragedy.

XXIV

Mine eye hath play'd the painter and hath stell'd,
Thy beauty's form in table of my heart;
My body is the frame wherein 'tis held,
And perspective it is best painter's art.
For through the painter must you see his skill,
To find where your true image pictur'd lies,
Which in my bosom's shop is hanging still,
That hath his windows glazed with thine eyes.
Now see what good turns eyes for eyes have done:
Mine eyes have drawn thy shape, and thine for me
Are windows to my breast, where-through the sun
Delights to peep, to gaze therein on thee;
  Yet eyes this cunning want to grace their art,
  They draw but what they see, know not the heart.

It doesn't matter that I cannot breathe
Conrad Kemp

There is nothing to be done. Nothing to
Be done, nothing to be done when the
Blood quickens, like,
No no, not that, but as, yes, as
A chemical dead attended by
Your pulse, your pulse, your silken, tempered pulse.

I wish my teeth were sharper and my clamp
Quicker. Precise, precise beyond
The practiced stroke of the money-man
Portraitist. Beyond the duress of the ancient addict.
The compulsion of my half-dead heart is
Undone by my harder, harder tissues.

So I draw you, not into my heart,
Simply to my gut, and I half-live
Another day.

XXV

Let those who are in favour with their stars
Of public honour and proud titles boast,
Whilst I, whom fortune of such triumph bars
Unlook'd for joy in that I honour most.
Great princes' favourites their fair leaves spread
But as the marigold at the sun's eye,
And in themselves their pride lies buried,
For at a frown they in their glory die.
The painful warrior famoused for fight,
After a thousand victories once foil'd,
Is from the book of honour razed quite,
And all the rest forgot for which he toil'd:
Then happy I, that love and am belov'd,
Where I may not remove nor be remov'd.

Perseids
Mark D. Cooper

for Jon

Dreaming or drunk, I walked the midnight road
beside the wood, as we had many times
after the pubs kicked out. A thin moon showed
the wood-lined, winding path to St. Kenelm's
graveyard where you, my always laughing friend,
were buried with a gun salute. Meteors
flared through low clouds, each incendiary
igniting dust-blooms like the spit of martyrs
and seen by me alone. Life is so brief.
I find a stray black rock and almost understand.
Buddha likened us to sparks but I believe
your star was a bright accident, and so
tonight the cool stone falls out of my hand.
The only love we have is letting go.

XXVI

Lord of my love, to whom in vassalage
Thy merit hath my duty strongly knit,
To thee I send this written embassage,
To witness duty, not to show my wit:
Duty so great, which wit so poor as mine
May make seem bare, in wanting words to show it,
But that I hope some good conceit of thine
In thy soul's thought, all naked, will bestow it:
Till whatsoever star that guides my moving,
Points on me graciously with fair aspect,
And puts apparel on my tatter'd loving,
To show me worthy of thy sweet respect:
  Then may I dare to boast how I do love thee;
  Till then, not show my head where thou mayst prove me.

Number 26
William Wyld

I think it's rude of you to ask but yes,
I'll admit it's double digits. I get
a lot of correspondence, mostly a mess
of abject poetry, apologies and threats.
I often sell the jewellery on but keep
the things I like to give to friends –
why not? The clutter makes it hard to sleep.
I see some post their stuff by hand, they tend
to come at dusk, grasping sadly at their
envelopes. Overcome with doubt one tried
to get his tawdry letter back, but the
heavy shutter of the letterbox prised
off his fingernail. Here, I keep it in
this velvet box. I gave away the ring.

XXVII

Weary with toil, I haste me to my bed,
The dear respose for limbs with travel tir'd;
But then begins a journey in my head
To work my mind, when body's work's expired:
For then my thoughts – from far where I abide –
Intend a zealous pilgrimage to thee,
And keep my drooping eyelids open wide,
Looking on darkness which the blind do see:
Save that my soul's imaginary sight
Presents thy shadow to my sightless view,
Which, like a jewel (hung in ghastly night,
Makes black night beauteous, and her old face new.
  Lo! thus, by day my limbs, by night my mind,
  For thee, and for myself, no quiet find.

After Sonnet XXVII *(four Centuries after)*
Pat Borthwick

At last! My bed. A bonus of clean sheets,
freshly-laundered pillowslips herb-scented
with thoughts of you, memories of kisses
up my spine, warm breath curling in my ear.
I'm dreaming four hundred years back to you
beyond sleep's horizon. I hear your voice
sparkling like a jewel in my deep darkness.
Sleep, you whisper. *Sleep.* And my eyes open,

open on fierce doubts shrouded in thick mist.
Suppose you were a dream and nothing more?
A cruel trick? Doors begin slamming shut.
Mute waterfalls turn into solid ice.
My bed clothes are faceted and frozen
until your words resound inside my head.

XXVIII

How can I then return in happy plight,
That am debarre'd the benefit of rest?
When day's oppression is not eas'd by night,
But day by night and night by day oppress'd,
And each, though enemies to either's reign,
Do in consent shake hands to torture me,
The one by toil, the other to complain
How far I toil, still farther off from thee.
I tell the day, to please him thou art bright,
And dost him grace when clouds do blot the heaven:
So flatter I the swart-complexion'd night,
When sparkling stars twire not thou gild'st the even.
　　But day doth daily draw my sorrows longer,
　　And night doth nightly make grief's length seem stronger.

'twixt
Anita Pati

Call this love? I'm whacked and dainty over u –
that pigeon heart has pestered me all year.
You Twitter in my ears a mating coo
and digitise your *Rati* everywhere.
My brain's not a computer yet it fires
a trillion cross-wired pings that sting of thee.
And when I work to block you out, my screen
spurts Facebook feeds that eat the nub of me.
I pick your pixelled face to breathe hard on,
I flatter flesh but then your seamy head
spirals into kitty snarls so I
start furrowing your golden forum threads.
I meditate I plead I flick you off
and still you grunt in me, no mind to stop.

XXIX

When in disgrace with fortune and men's eyes
I all alone beweep my outcast state,
And trouble deaf heaven with my bootless cries,
And look upon myself, and curse my fate,
Wishing me like to one more rich in hope,
Featur'd like him, like him with friends possess'd,
Desiring this man's art, and that man's scope,
With what I most enjoy contented least;
Yet in these thoughts my self almost despising,
Haply I think on thee, – and then my state,
Like to the lark at break of day arising
From sullen earth, sings hymns at heaven's gate;
  For thy sweet love remember'd such wealth brings
  That then I scorn to change my state with kings.

29
Oliver Mantell

No matter the hours I'm stranded on the phone
failing to reach a human through the menus;
the long days I work, long nights I'm home alone;
how many months our balance falls past zero;
no matter that I cannot understand
how others found an empire on LinkedIn,
afford their long-haul flights, or pension plan,
have confidence in what they will pass on:
no matter how early, you only want to play,
ride hobby-horses, dance with hats and hankies,
exhaust me long before the working day
with songs and smiles and tickles and tea with teddies.
And yet you make-believe me of my best:
'I'm the king of the castle!'. Yes.

XXX

When to the sessions of sweet silent thought
I summon up remembrance of things past,
I sigh the lack of many a thing I sought,
And with old woes new wail my dear time's waste:
Then can I drown an eye, unused to flow,
For precious friends hid in death's dateless night,
And weep afresh love's long since cancell'd woe,
And moan the expense of many a vanish'd sight:
Then can I grieve at grievances foregone,
And heavily from woe to woe tell o'er
The sad account of fore-bemoaned moan,
Which I new pay as if not paid before.
 But if the while I think on thee, dear friend,
 All losses are restor'd and sorrows end.

Invitation
Mike Di Placido

One day
it *will* happen –
that Italian feast in the garden:

long tables
under pergolas
clustered with grapes;

pasta, vino, dancing
and music – oh yes – *definitely* music;
Gigli, Pavarotti *and* Sinatra, capisce?

But most importantly, on the guest list, you.

And when the stragglers
are laughing down the lane
to their taxis and cars,

we'll sit
by the little gnarled apple tree,
as thudding moths shake the lanterns,

and I'll thank you, then,
with the backing of the open heavens
until the dying of the last star.

XXXI

Thy bosom is endeared with all hearts,
Which I by lacking have supposed dead;
And there reigns Love, and all Love's loving parts,
And all those friends which I thought buried.
How many a holy and obsequious tear
Hath dear religious love stol'n from mine eye,
As interest of the dead, which now appear
But things remov'd that hidden in thee lie!
Thou art the grave where buried love doth live,
Hung with the trophies of my lovers gone,
Who all their parts of me to thee did give,
That due of many now is thine alone:
  Their images I lov'd, I view in thee,
  And thou – all they – hast all the all of me.

Sonnet XXXI (b)
Eoghan Walls

So love might be understood as light-in-flesh,
illuminating us the way a torch makes pink a fist,
the same way the sea's light holds up a jellyfish.
Observe, for example, the firefly heart of Christ,
flickering and buzzing over the translucent skin
of a dying nun, promising such bioluminescence
as would enflame her like a candle in a pumpkin.
Such love is not the sole property of the reverent.

Consider yourself now, sunbathing in the park
with your t-shirt rolled up, and how our foetus
stretches in the glow of your near-opaque heart,
your liver's greys, suspended like stained glass,
as love permeates the red cathedrals of your skin
that I would enter, that you would hold me in.

XXXII

If thou survive my well-contented day,
When that churl Death my bones with dust shall cover
And shalt by fortune once more re-survey
These poor rude lines of thy deceased lover,
Compare them with the bett'ring of the time,
And though they be outstripp'd by every pen,
Reserve them for my love, not for their rhyme,
Exceeded by the height of happier men.
O! then vouchsafe me but this loving thought:
'Had my friend's Muse grown with this growing age,
A dearer birth than this his love had brought,
To march in ranks of better equipage:
  But since he died and poets better prove,
  Theirs for their style I'll read, his for his love'.

32
Becky Edwards

And yet it's you survives me; far beyond
The feeble dust that Death laid on your grave,
Your words have gathered quickly to abscond
From mouldy silence. Fled their muffled cave,
Where unmarked minds lie gently growing dim,
They shimmer now in glory through the earth
To spill their light on pages. Yes, those grim
Set ranks of stone-faced poets know their worth.
Still one soft reader, loving, turns to bless
The contours of your face in every line.
Were your skill dull, had your great art been less,
Those words eked out in quiet would be mine.
    Yet the whole world knows them and, unmoved,
    Reserves them for their rhyme and not your love.

XXXIII

Full many a glorious morning have I seen
Flatter the mountain tops with sovereign eye,
Kissing with golden face the meadows green,
Gilding pale streams with heavenly alchemy;
Anon permit the basest clouds to ride
With ugly rack on his celestial face,
And from the forlorn world his visage hide,
Stealing unseen to west with this disgrace:
Even so my sun one early morn did shine,
With all triumphant splendour on my brow;
But out! alack! he was but one hour mine,
The region cloud hath mask'd him from me now.
  Yet him for this my love no whit disdaineth;
  Suns of the world may stain when heaven's sun staineth.

Southampton in Paris
Matt Barnard

The Queen commands me back in London, but I
have four Queens here that demand my attention
four Queens to pair with four Kings, if only
luck would play his part. This table's battlefield
is all I need, and drink and willing girls.

Why think about tomorrow, with its chances fickle
as the dice and cards? Screw it all, screw friends
screw wives in Fleet, screw the Dowager Countess
and her late-flowering lust, screw the court's pet,
that gentleman always ready with a sly word.

To all those who need me, I say find another.
To all those who want me, love another.
What do I owe to any man or to any state,
what do I care if I lose my hand or head?
Let all that stinking country go to hell -

O, I know, the 'wright, the 'wright, the 'wright!

XXXIV

Why didst thou promise such a beauteous day,
And make me travel forth without my cloak,
To let base clouds o'ertake me in my way,
Hiding thy bravery in their rotten smoke?
'Tis not enough that through the cloud thou break,
To dry the rain on my storm-beaten face,
For no man well of such a salve can speak,
That heals the wound, and cures not the disgrace:
Nor can thy shame give physic to my grief;
Though thou repent, yet I have still the loss:
The offender's sorrow lends but weak relief
To him that bears the strong offence's cross.
  Ah! but those tears are pearl which thy love sheds,
  And they are rich and ransom all ill deeds.

Response to Sonnet 34
Marilyn Daish

They walked the shoreline curve,
the warm abandonment of their hands
folded against intrusion.

'With you to the ends of the Earth,' He said.
A fidget by the wall, he crept towards the door,
slammed on his careless dissection of her life.
Trace elements left behind in the drift of its parts,
a broken chair, upturned table, her heart.

The sincerity of his tears repaid his debt.
She pocketed them against her loss.

The kitchen warm. The table set.
Her tea is white, no sugar.
His black.
She is out of milk.

She picks up her umbrella,
closes the door.
A winter sun drops its pale cast
behind a bruised cloud,
dissolving her shadow.
Rain spots her cupped palms,
escapes between fingers.

Wrapped tight in her mac,
her head retreats within its hood
against the seep of winter.

XXXV

No more be griev'd at that which thou hast done:
Roses have thorns, and silver fountains mud:
Clouds and eclipses stain both moon and sun,
And loathsome canker lives in sweetest bud.
All men make faults, and even I in this,
Authorizing thy trespass with compare,
Myself corrupting, salving thy amiss,
Excusing thy sins more than thy sins are;
For to thy sensual fault I bring in sense, –
Thy adverse party is thy advocate, –
And 'gainst myself a lawful plea commence:
Such civil war is in my love and hate,
  That I an accessary needs must be,
  To that sweet thief which sourly robs from me.

Two Voices
Charles Evans

It was a small absence
and small the words from the far place,
the card with the hurried writing,
the details that didn't matter,
and the squeezed name
by the smudged kiss in the corner, consoling

It was a short trip
and short my time alone in the house.
When the phone rang I snatched it like a child,
just made it, the awaited call,
quick greetings, the news, plans,
the one voice hot in my ear, thrilling

It was fast talk
and fast my question gabbled *Do you miss me?*
On the distant line I caught her voice,
pictured the scene far off,
views, visits, adventures,
the mood known and familiar, rushing

I heard the last goodbye
– only not the last words.
The line still open, and
He makes such a fuss if I don't
and the giggle of girls together, betraying

XXXVI

Let me confess that we two must be twain,
Although our undivided loves are one:
So shall those blots that do with me remain,
Without thy help, by me be borne alone.
In our two loves there is but one respect,
Though in our lives a separable spite,
Which though it alter not love's sole effect,
Yet doth it steal sweet hours from love's delight.
I may not evermore acknowledge thee,
Lest my bewailed guilt should do thee shame,
Nor thou with public kindness honour me,
Unless thou take that honour from thy name:
  But do not so, I love thee in such sort,
  As thou being mine, mine is thy good report.

36
Sue Wrinch

You are beyond my league so we must part,
I am grounded, you fly upwards spirit-winged.
but if we could pretend equality, shut out
public gaze, exist in space between a blink,
in the blackness of an eye and sweep of lid,
we would be together still, outside time.

We are in fame unequal, your feet ride high
and clear in air, mine drag in dust and blur.
I will bear my faults alone, yet still I yearn,
quiver like water in the wind, for you are
like a pendulum swung by me just out of
reach, and out of reach again.

You will not show me public kindness nor
I acknowledge you, lest my shame stains.
But no, for my reputation grows and its silk
can cover both with lustre. Our differences,
like minerals trapped in strata will combine
and slowly form as crystals caught in time.

XXXVII

As a decrepit father takes delight
To see his active child do deeds of youth,
So I, made lame by Fortune's dearest spite,
Take all my comfort of thy worth and truth;
For whether beauty, birth, or wealth, or wit,
Or any of these all, or all, or more,
Entitled in thy parts, do crowned sit,
I make my love engrafted, to this store:
So then I am not lame, poor, nor despis'd,
Whilst that this shadow doth such substance give
That I in thy abundance am suffic'd,
And by a part of all thy glory live.
  Look what is best, that best I wish in thee:
  This wish I have; then ten times happy me!

37
Nick MacKinnon

Or not. Consider Ronald Reagan who
life-guarded on Rock River, Illinois,
and rescued scores of women, one or two
repeatedly. Well, Ronnie had a boy
(with Nancy), and he named the youngster Ron
to save confusion. Every summer they
would swim a two-length race which Ronnie won
in Californian style. At puberty
Ron joined his high school swim team, where he'd learn
to tumble. Next race, level at the turn,
Ronnie was old-school tucked while Ron had flipped,
and hard as Ronnie swam, Ron fingertipped.
"You cheated!" was the Governor's refrain,
and Ron and Ronnie never swam again.

XXXVIII

How can my muse want subject to invent,
While thou dost breathe, that pour'st into my verse
Thine own sweet argument, too excellent
For every vulgar paper to rehearse?
O! give thy self the thanks, if aught in me
Worthy perusal stand against thy sight;
For who's so dumb that cannot write to thee,
When thou thy self dost give invention light?
Be thou the tenth Muse, ten times more in worth
Than those old nine which rhymers invocate;
And he that calls on thee, let him bring forth
Eternal numbers to outlive long date.
  If my slight muse do please these curious days,
  The pain be mine, but thine shall be the praise.

38
Sophie Reynolds

You are not short of inspiration
for, you say, my eyes and lips
provide the spark to send
a thousand poems thundering
around your heart. And yet
these pages you present
are bare, unmarked,
white as a winter morning
that's untrodden yet.
The poetry you promised me
was never writ;
your love may burn forever
but your words do not.

XXXIX

O! how thy worth with manners may I sing,
When thou art all the better part of me?
What can mine own praise to mine own self bring?
And what is't but mine own when I praise thee?
Even for this, let us divided live,
And our dear love lose name of single one,
That by this separation I may give
That due to thee which thou deserv'st alone.
O absence! what a torment wouldst thou prove,
Were it not thy sour leisure gave sweet leave,
To entertain the time with thoughts of love,
Which time and thoughts so sweetly doth deceive,
  And that thou teachest how to make one twain,
  By praising him here who doth hence remain.

Ivy Seeds
Arji Manuelpillai

You sprinkled ivy seeds as you left me
watered and nurtured, planted with naive eyes
propped on bamboo dug deep into my foot.
The sprout shot unsurprisingly quickly.

It ascended, piano fingered, inch by inch
fitting into holes I had forgotten existed
weathering into unfilled Romeo steps.
I lived waiting, waiting to live.

It grew with a trail of painted words
worn in my hair, like cans from wedding cars
intertwining you into every action
'til every reaction was tempered by you.

It crawled between the bricks of what used to be me
over windows and doors, floors and balcony seats
'til i forgot the shades that made me me.
'til these walls would tumble without you there.

Then, in the darkness of a breezeless winter
I saw it change but noticed not when.
Extracting remnants of me as it perished.
No answer. Piles of inanimate remains.

You, the greatest part of me.

Gone.

XL

Take all my loves, my love, yea take them all;
What hast thou then more than thou hadst before?
No love, my love, that thou mayst true love call;
All mine was thine, before thou hadst this more.
Then, if for my love, thou my love receivest,
I cannot blame thee, for my love thou usest;
But yet be blam'd, if thou thy self deceivest
By wilful taste of what thyself refusest.
I do forgive thy robbery, gentle thief,
Although thou steal thee all my poverty:
And yet, love knows it is a greater grief
To bear love's wrong, than hate's known injury.
  Lascivious grace, in whom all ill well shows,
  Kill me with spites yet we must not be foes.

3 p.m.
Iain Batchelor

Though never old, the sheets we slid into
were always never new. A welcome worthy
of our stolen three p.m's. You remind me-
soiled sheets for soiled minds.

Though it was always day, the tired drapes stayed
louchely un-ironed and drawn. To prying fishwife eyes,
an open window offered saucy little preludes,
observed cups of hurried tea.

But we got to it. We were never seen. Over. And over again.

Though never present, the heart of him
dribbled timidly on the floor. The molten band
cauterising your finger,
where the sin threatened to spill out.

Though I left on time, my clean clothes concealing
my damp worked-over frame. He meets me
at your door. His hand to my shoulder-
How was work? I say, *Fine-*
and we forget where I was before.

XLI

Those pretty wrongs that liberty commits,
When I am sometime absent from thy heart,
Thy beauty, and thy years full well befits,
For still temptation follows where thou art.
Gentle thou art, and therefore to be won,
Beauteous thou art, therefore to be assail'd;
And when a woman woos, what woman's son
Will sourly leave her till he have prevail'd?
Ay me! but yet thou mightst my seat forbear,
And chide thy beauty and thy straying youth,
Who lead thee in their riot even there
Where thou art forced to break a twofold truth: –
  Hers by thy beauty tempting her to thee,
  Thine by thy beauty being false to me.

Sonnet 41 take two
Gordon Fudge

So fellah. Dude
You're shaggin' my bird, yeah?
Bothered? Do I look bothered?
I. Am. Not. Bothered.
Ok so I am a bit bothered.
But look. You're a good lookin' guy
What bird couldn't resist you?
Not my bird. Clearly.
And look. She came after you.
So not your fault right?
Like I say.
You're a looker. Really buff.
You are the Buffmeister
Doctor Buffenstein
Buffy the cuckold slayer.
Quite fancy you myself
To be honest.
Anyway.
Good on yer.
Have fun. And er.
Gimme a bell sometime?
Maybe?
Take care, yeah?

XLII

That thou hast her it is not all my grief,
And yet it may be said I loved her dearly;
That she hath thee is of my wailing chief,
A loss in love that touches me more nearly.
Loving offenders thus I will excuse ye:
Thou dost love her, because thou know'st I love her;
And for my sake even so doth she abuse me,
Suffering my friend for my sake to approve her.
If I lose thee, my loss is my love's gain,
And losing her, my friend hath found that loss;
Both find each other, and I lose both twain,
And both for my sake lay on me this cross:
  But here's the joy; my friend and I are one;
  Sweet flattery! then she loves but me alone.

42

Graham Goddard

I stare into the mirror of the bathroom cabinet

Swigs

The thought of her with him grabs my attention cleverly

Gargles

He is a better man but that man is me

Spits

You him, him her, you me

Rinse

Three stare into the mirror of the bathroom cabinet

Only two, stare back

XLIII

When most I wink, then do mine eyes best see,
For all the day they view things unrespected;
But when I sleep, in dreams they look on thee,
And darkly bright, are bright in dark directed.
Then thou, whose shadow shadows doth make bright,
How would thy shadow's form form happy show
To the clear day with thy much clearer light,
When to unseeing eyes thy shade shines so!
How would, I say, mine eyes be blessed made
By looking on thee in the living day,
When in dead night thy fair imperfect shade
Through heavy sleep on sightless eyes doth stay!
  All days are nights to see till I see thee,
  And nights bright days when dreams do show thee me.

I see you when I wink
PJ Heinz

It's been a long time.

When I picture you now…
The image is really just

One of the photos in the album.
Not an actual memory.

Then, sometimes, when
I least expect it, you walk

Into a dream. Unannounced
Unexplained. Just there

In the middle of a scene,
A breathing anachronism.

Waking widows me again.

XLIV

If the dull substance of my flesh were thought,
Injurious distance should not stop my way;
For then despite of space I would be brought,
From limits far remote, where thou dost stay.
No matter then although my foot did stand
Upon the farthest earth remov'd from thee;
For nimble thought can jump both sea and land,
As soon as think the place where he would be.
But, ah! thought kills me that I am not thought,
To leap large lengths of miles when thou art gone,
But that so much of earth and water wrought,
I must attend time's leisure with my moan;
  Receiving nought by elements so slow
  But heavy tears, badges of either's woe.

Sonnet on Distance
Robert Powell

After Shakespeare's XLIV
'If the dull substance of my flesh were thought'

I thought I knew I loved, and distances would prove it true.
That Fall I jumped the sea alone, landed, but thought of you;
then, when you came, took lengths again to move away
and missed you, though thought it right we were apart!
Where my body was without, my thoughts were with you;
when with you, thoughts leapt the sea, or went knowingly
across miles to land's ends.   This changed:
I came to think thoughts and flesh in one place should be,
returned, collapsed the thousand miles of thought to touch
your summer cheek, which turned its face away from me.
Not only land and sea, water, earth, time, but thought itself,
plays miles out in the space we let between our selves.
    What's distant can't be caught. I should have felt,
    and held, what far inside I'd known and thought.

XLV

The other two, slight air, and purging fire
Are both with thee, wherever I abide;
The first my thought, the other my desire,
These present-absent with swift motion slide.
For when these quicker elements are gone
In tender embassy of love to thee,
My life, being made of four, with two alone
Sinks down to death, oppress'd with melancholy;
Until life's composition be recur'd
By those swift messengers return'd from thee,
Who even but now come back again, assur'd,
Of thy fair health, recounting it to me:
  This told, I joy; but then no longer glad,
  I send them back again, and straight grow sad.

45
James Nash

We hold between us all four elements
Which bind us even in our times apart,
Love and friendship, tight ravelled filaments,
Strong wires which knit as one our beating heart.
Sometime when you're away I dreaming sit,
And imagine a world if you were not,
And if my dream is deep I can forget,
Those humours which we share, the lanyard knot.
We players can be lovers or be fools,
Phlegmatic in the journeys made since birth,
Can shape and sculpt the air to our own rules,
One may be fire, the other may choose earth.
This contract is such, that none can impeach,
Both sanguine in the love we have for each.

XLVI

Mine eye and heart are at a mortal war,
How to divide the conquest of thy sight;
Mine eye my heart thy picture's sight would bar,
My heart mine eye the freedom of that right.
My heart doth plead that thou in him dost lie, –
A closet never pierc'd with crystal eyes –
But the defendant doth that plea deny,
And says in him thy fair appearance lies.
To side this title is impannelled
A quest of thoughts, all tenants to the heart;
And by their verdict is determined
The clear eye's moiety, and the dear heart's part:
  As thus; mine eye's due is thy outward part,
  And my heart's right, thy inward love of heart.

Truth proves thievish
Kelley Swain

Do not trust the historian.
All of him is borrowed or stolen:
The turned-up collar: Sherlock Holmes.
The jokes: Jeeves & Wooster.
The love lines: Woody Allen. He'll say:
"Darling, this is *our* city," in each city.
Childhood memories, (so-called,) fall,
Verbatim, from books on his shelf.

Even his sins are unoriginal.

Do not trust the historian:
All of him is borrowed or stolen.
His walls are bricks of books,
Facts recycled and retold.
He's only safe in tales of old.

XLVII

Betwixt mine eye and heart a league is took,
And each doth good turns now unto the other:
When that mine eye is famish'd for a look,
Or heart in love with sighs himself doth smother,
With my love's picture then my eye doth feast,
And to the painted banquet bids my heart;
Another time mine eye is my heart's guest,
And in his thoughts of love doth share a part:
So, either by thy picture or my love,
Thy self away, art present still with me;
For thou not farther than my thoughts canst move,
And I am still with them, and they with thee;
  Or, if they sleep, thy picture in my sight
  Awakes my heart, to heart's and eye's delight.

Sonnet for Julian and Frances
Jo Reed Turner

Remember that photograph they took
just as you two, smiling, looked
away from each other, glanced
toward the friends who smothered
you in white confetti before the feast?
My heart faltered a little that day -
the uninvited guest, but knew
that though our lives would be lived apart
it would not lessen the profound love
I felt for you, that you professed for me.
I framed the portrait, and when I moved
hung it there on the wall in constant sight,
and when I recall our dovetailed pasts
its always with infinite sweet delight.

XLVIII

How careful was I when I took my way,
Each trifle under truest bars to thrust,
That to my use it might unused stay
From hands of falsehood, in sure wards of trust!
But thou, to whom my jewels trifles are,
Most worthy comfort, now my greatest grief,
Thou best of dearest, and mine only care,
Art left the prey of every vulgar thief.
Thee have I not lock'd up in any chest,
Save where thou art not, though I feel thou art,
Within the gentle closure of my breast,
From whence at pleasure thou mayst come and part;
　And even thence thou wilt be stol'n I fear,
　For truth proves thievish for a prize so dear.

Perfect Security
Richard O'Brien

The story of the combination lock
is ultimately one of opening.
Millennia of cleanly stolen stock
keyed up the intricately fumbled thing
held to your ear. Shake it, if you must —
the closest earthly analogue to safe —
and hear the heavy industry of trust,
the steady, precise tumblers of faith.
We build aware that what we build will break,
that we're a hairpin's breadth from dissolution,
knowing the transplant might not ever take,
that there are problems which have no solution.
　　To hold still, though you hold imperfectly,
　　I hold our only true security.

XLIX

Against that time, if ever that time come,
When I shall see thee frown on my defects,
When as thy love hath cast his utmost sum,
Call'd to that audit by advis'd respects;
Against that time when thou shalt strangely pass,
And scarcely greet me with that sun, thine eye,
When love, converted from the thing it was,
Shall reasons find of settled gravity;
Against that time do I ensconce me here,
Within the knowledge of mine own desert,
And this my hand, against my self uprear,
To guard the lawful reasons on thy part:
　To leave poor me thou hast the strength of laws,
　Since why to love I can allege no cause.

Krakatoa Moon
Liane Strauss

Until that time, which you say will not come,
When one of us, or both, or none accepts
That we don't feel the way, or depth, or sum
Of what we want to feel, with few regrets;
Until that time when I see you pretend,
Or feel myself at odds with my own will,
Pronouncing words that palliate or send
The truth under the tread of love's true wheel;
Until that time I'll toe the lover's line
And we will live like islands on a fault
Where tremors sing until they are a sign
Of your reproach for my backstabbing thought:
For I'm the earth the tide the moon the sun
And you will be destroyed by what I've done.

L

How heavy do I journey on the way,
When what I seek, my weary travel's end,
Doth teach that ease and that repose to say,
'Thus far the miles are measured from thy friend!'
The beast that bears me, tired with my woe,
Plods dully on, to bear that weight in me,
As if by some instinct the wretch did know
His rider lov'd not speed, being made from thee:
The bloody spur cannot provoke him on,
That sometimes anger thrusts into his hide,
Which heavily he answers with a groan,
More sharp to me than spurring to his side;
  For that same groan doth put this in my mind,
  My grief lies onward, and my joy behind.

Closing the Door
Bill Haugse

For L.

I'm standing in your doorway now
unleashed, a dog baffled by freedom
boxes already in my trunk, and the wax fruit

I'll return when you're not here
for the red chair, rug
You keep the couch
you seem to need it
to sleep on

We'd planned a little drink between
these acts and my setting out
But you've managed two excuses
I retaliate with one of my own
mine the more credible
neither true

We stop, but you turn away
my eyes might see the
juggled rage? green flecks
of something like love

Soon I'll see street lights
crawling up my splattered
windshield, the jazz station
full blast, wondering whether
you've stayed in or gone out
perhaps driven to the sea
shout secrets against the tide

LI

Thus can my love excuse the slow offence
Of my dull bearer when from thee I speed:
From where thou art why should I haste me thence?
Till I return, of posting is no need.
O! what excuse will my poor beast then find,
When swift extremity can seem but slow?
Then should I spur, though mounted on the wind,
In winged speed no motion shall I know,
Then can no horse with my desire keep pace;
Therefore desire, of perfect'st love being made,
Shall neigh – no dull flesh – in his fiery race;
But love, for love, thus shall excuse my jade, –
  'Since from thee going, he went wilful-slow,
  Towards thee I'll run, and give him leave to go.'

51
David Bowe

Unsure how to settle in these rhythms of distance
I've slept more miles than I've travelled
with you / eaten horizons alone
when altitude allows the sun in for longer
when degrees more than miles measure space
but returns are a matter of boarding
cards and leave to remain
and to go, which amounts to the same.

And we wait.

I'm flying soon and this is enough,
home soon and this is enough
to instil patience, buy the in-between
days on other soil, the wrong side of the road,
the ocean and hope
we might fly together next time, and return.

LII

So am I as the rich, whose blessed key,
Can bring him to his sweet up-locked treasure,
The which he will not every hour survey,
For blunting the fine point of seldom pleasure.
Therefore are feasts so solemn and so rare,
Since, seldom coming in that long year set,
Like stones of worth they thinly placed are,
Or captain jewels in the carcanet.
So is the time that keeps you as my chest,
Or as the wardrobe which the robe doth hide,
To make some special instant special-blest,
By new unfolding his imprison'd pride.
  Blessed are you whose worthiness gives scope,
  Being had, to triumph; being lacked, to hope.

On Sonnet 52
Francesco Aresco

I am as the rich here where I live,
my talents are many, my treasures too.
my sight is good for beauties and colours,
my hearing catches the song and the chord,
my blood runs fast, my hair is tick.
Frequently I have the laugh of the hour,
the pleasure I seek is always before me.

But when the rustle of night's robe
and swishing clouds come at my silent bed
the sky breaks down and the truth I know.
My eye makes me blind,
my ear makes me deaf,
my arteries and veins are cruel ropes,
worse! seaweed drowning me down.

And so I pray to see my scope
in its silent lack I triumph in hope.

LIII

What is your substance, whereof are you made,
That millions of strange shadows on you tend?
Since every one, hath every one, one shade,
And you but one, can every shadow lend.
Describe Adonis, and the counterfeit
Is poorly imitated after you;
On Helen's cheek all art of beauty set,
And you in Grecian tires are painted new:
Speak of the spring, and foison of the year,
The one doth shadow of your beauty show,
The other as your bounty doth appear;
And you in every blessed shape we know.
  In all external grace you have some part,
  But you like none, none you, for constant heart.

53
Mark Leech

Is your true substance of dark matter made?
Unmeasurable unless looked at slant:
shadow's shadow calculation, the real
a bounty written out in numbers.
        You share so many genes with everything
you are a holotype of life: all green,
all that spores, divides, that feeds, grows and breeds
exists in you, your tissues, webs and threads.
        So hidden, so interleaved, your substance
casts no shadow – or is all shadow – or
is lit by the energy of what is:
on every wavelength, illumination.
        Your art is, to be distilled of all things
and yet to give them name and history.

LIV

O! how much more doth beauty beauteous seem
By that sweet ornament which truth doth give.
The rose looks fair, but fairer we it deem
For that sweet odour, which doth in it live.
The canker blooms have full as deep a dye
As the perfumed tincture of the roses.
Hang on such thorns, and play as wantonly
When summer's breath their masked buds discloses:
But, for their virtue only is their show,
They live unwoo'd, and unrespected fade;
Die to themselves. Sweet roses do not so;
Of their sweet deaths, are sweetest odours made:
  And so of you, beauteous and lovely youth,
  When that shall vade, by verse distills your truth.

Rose
Anthony Fisher

Your truth, is chemistry.
Your beauteous red, anthocyanin.
Your sweet odour eugenol, farnesol,
geraniol, linalool, farnesol, nerol.
But my truth, eddying around my neurons
my heart overwhelmed as I woo you?
I bathe in deep dye from velveteen petals
spin in your sweet summer's breath
born of fragrance and innocent blushes
of the nymph pursued and loved by Dionysus.
So moved was he, that he took these,
transformed them to wanton blooms
to ever hang on this thorny bush
that had rent her clothes, pricked her.

LV

Not marble, nor the gilded monuments
Of princes, shall outlive this powerful rhyme;
But you shall shine more bright in these contents
Than unswept stone, besmear'd with sluttish time.
When wasteful war shall statues overturn,
And broils root out the work of masonry,
Nor Mars his sword, nor war's quick fire shall burn
The living record of your memory.
'Gainst death, and all-oblivious enmity
Shall you pace forth; your praise shall still find room
Even in the eyes of all posterity
That wear this world out to the ending doom.
  So, till the judgment that yourself arise,
  You live in this, and dwell in lovers' eyes.

forget it
Edwina Attlee

We shall move
and the doorframes forget us
we shall move and
our children will tell us they are hungry
we shall move
and remember our dreams.
Waiting in the corridor holding pink skirt between two
fingers thinking why did I choose
this one? And in the other room light making spectacles
of the walls.
And pineapples!
Sweet press of sweat to fabric
and sweat to flesh
and flesh to flesh
because? Oh wake up!

LVI

Sweet love, renew thy force; be it not said
Thy edge should blunter be than appetite,
Which but to-day by feeding is allay'd,
To-morrow sharpened in his former might:
So, love, be thou, although to-day thou fill
Thy hungry eyes, even till they wink with fulness,
To-morrow see again, and do not kill
The spirit of love, with a perpetual dulness.
Let this sad interim like the ocean be
Which parts the shore, where two contracted new
Come daily to the banks, that when they see
Return of love, more blest may be the view;
  Or call it winter, which being full of care,
  Makes summer's welcome, thrice more wished, more rare.

Fast and Feast
David Underdown

Desire comes as a surprise, a quickening
of the senses: a curve beneath a blouse,
a fingertip, then that familiar thickening
of the blood no common-sense will douse.
If afterwards our moods subside again
and slip into the same too well-worn groove
we should not worry. Why try to feign
passion, as if there's something we must prove?
For you and I, my sweet, know how to feast
and when to fast. The keenest appetite
comes from abstention: so wait while love's yeast
leavens, from dull dough, bread that will delight,
and make, on perfect mornings, all sleep past,
the finest meal of all, breakfast – *break fast.*

LVII

Being your slave what should I do but tend,
Upon the hours, and times of your desire?
I have no precious time at all to spend;
Nor services to do, till you require.
Nor dare I chide the world-without-end hour,
Whilst I, my sovereign, watch the clock for you,
Nor think the bitterness of absence sour,
When you have bid your servant once adieu;
Nor dare I question with my jealous thought
Where you may be, or your affairs suppose,
But, like a sad slave, stay and think of nought
Save, where you are, how happy you make those.
  So true a fool is love, that in your will,
  Though you do anything, he thinks no ill.

Frenzy
Matt Riker

Whilst I, my sovereign, watch the clock for you

Each place its own inventory of loss.
I glimpse your face in the crowd
and look again — there is a stranger

wearing it. In the chatter of the cafés
I hear your voice, in the whine of cooling vents
and in the humming of the wires.

Rush hour at the station. I'm startled
by your perfume. In vain I search
for you among the passengers.

Your breath is in my bloodstream.
It hovers on my lips. I see you
half reflected in a window.

After we parted, your scent
still stayed a while on my skin.
Impermanent tattoo of frankincense.

Happy he who forgets. I create:
failed distractions, taxonomies
for pain. It's time — I close my eyes

and on the inside of my eyelids
slowly let your face dissolve.

LVIII

That god forbid, that made me first your slave,
I should in thought control your times of pleasure,
Or at your hand the account of hours to crave,
Being your vassal, bound to stay your leisure!
O! let me suffer, being at your beck,
The imprison'd absence of your liberty;
And patience, tame to sufferance, bide each check,
Without accusing you of injury.
Be where you list, your charter is so strong
That you yourself may privilage your time
To what you will; to you it doth belong
Yourself to pardon of self-doing crime.
  I am to wait, though waiting so be hell,
  Not blame your pleasure be it ill or well.

Self-Help Advice
Antony Mair

When I unclip their leads, the dogs are off -
sniffing for rabbits, chasing birds across
the scented hillside in the fixed belief
they're wolves in pursuit of prey, lost in the bliss
    of an atavistic chase.

But they'll return as fast, remembering
that food rewards obedience. They hear
my call, race back and stare with longing
at the ready treat. Their hunt's less sure
    than good behaviour.

You have no dogs, since otherwise you'd know
that instinct's curbed by knowledge. There's no sense
in letting go and waiting – you must show
the reward for staying, so that he discounts
    what now appear constraints.

Forget this talk of slaves and vassals. Try
to teach him where his interest lies. Don't beg.
But if he's foolish, and chooses to play away,
don't hesitate – dismiss him as a rogue
    and get yourself a dog.

LIX

If there be nothing new, but that which is
Hath been before, how are our brains beguil'd,
Which labouring for invention bear amiss
The second burthen of a former child!
O! that record could with a backward look,
Even of five hundred courses of the sun,
Show me your image in some antique book,
Since mind at first in character was done!
That I might see what the old world could say
To this composed wonder of your frame;
Wh'r we are mended, or wh'r better they,
Or whether revolution be the same.
  O! sure I am the wits of former days,
  To subjects worse have given admiring praise.

parks and creation
Matthew Stoppard

under the rustling of baking parchment where
Sunday and bread dough is brought to its knees
he hears a radio sermon calling to those days
hymn and hiccups over boiled eggs and soldiers:
a backwoods youth taught to tell time by the sun
takes his turn as shaman of public parks
a drake's quack and greylag's honk for the wife
who came waddling up - courting is chasing tail
where he comes from   nevermind how much hair
or teeth fall out or how grace gave way to motherhood
and a heel-toe gait punishing their floorboards;
romance moults a little more each year
yet feathers fly when they dive in bedside light
heads hitting the pillow at the same time

LX

Like as the waves make towards the pebbled shore,
So do our minutes hasten to their end;
Each changing place with that which goes before,
In sequent toil all forwards do contend.
Nativity, once in the main of light,
Crawls to maturity, wherewith being crown'd,
Crooked eclipses 'gainst his glory fight,
And Time that gave doth now his gift confound.
Time doth transfix the flourish set on youth
And delves the parallels in beauty's brow,
Feeds on the rarities of nature's truth,
And nothing stands but for his scythe to mow:
  And yet to times in hope, my verse shall stand.
  Praising thy worth, despite his cruel hand.

Time, Ladies and Gentlemen, Please
Mark Fiddes

Time's back tapping that empty pint with nails.
Bar stool Falstaff, he raps out the seconds
Like he's the one who thirsts another round,
Not you, not here, not now and knowing how
Your lot is hocked, long pawned on tick, on tock.
Watch those fingers thick as cheap sausages
Mark every minute with a hollow knock,
Unlike his pale brother who gloves both hands
The better to disguise the scything scars.
Time won't give a toss what you think of him;
This last hour's glass he's poured in wrack and sand
Served with a pebble to salt the palate,
While the jukebox plays Knights in White Satin
Never reaching the end, Time and again.

LXI

Is it thy will, thy image should keep open
My heavy eyelids to the weary night?
Dost thou desire my slumbers should be broken,
While shadows like to thee do mock my sight?
Is it thy spirit that thou send'st from thee
So far from home into my deeds to pry,
To find out shames and idle hours in me,
The scope and tenure of thy jealousy?
O, no! thy love, though much, is not so great:
It is my love that keeps mine eye awake:
Mine own true love that doth my rest defeat,
To play the watchman ever for thy sake:
  For thee watch I, whilst thou dost wake elsewhere,
  From me far off, with others all too near.

61
Stephen Sharkey

I was seventeen (or maybe eighteen) when
I heard that Northern actor (Barrie Rutter?)
Play the watchman in the celebrated NT
Production of the Oresteia, Tony
Harrison's fantastic, muscular
Poetry. I saw it in my sixth form

Classics class. On VHS. I'd never
Been to London. And I'd never kissed a girl
(or anyone else). God knows I dreamed
About it. Day and night. It was the world.
And I knew from books and plays that when I did
I'd burn like Troy. And I couldn't wait.

"Come on, blasted beacon!
Blaze out of the blackness!"

LXII

Sin of self-love possesseth all mine eye
And all my soul, and all my every part;
And for this sin there is no remedy,
It is so grounded inward in my heart.
Methinks no face so gracious is as mine,
No shape so true, no truth of such account;
And for myself mine own worth do define,
As I all other in all worths surmount.
But when my glass shows me myself indeed
Beated and chopp'd with tanned antiquity,
Mine own self-love quite contrary I read;
Self so self-loving were iniquity.
  'Tis thee, – myself, – that for myself I praise,
  Painting my age with beauty of thy days.

LXII IIXL
JL Williams

It's hard to admit eye never loved I,
startled from a womb-scarred body to start
learning the ways this body is not free —
horse tied to horse tied to horse tied to cart.
I stare into a mirrored face that pines,
odd, craving eyes whose love I can't discount
and all for them my own fears I decline.
Their silence and their stillness tantamount,
were hers the species of face that could bleed
she might comprehend the absurdity
of a woman's life stratified by need
and a powerful — painful clarity.
     As I burn she enters a lighter phase;
     warm, warming as the sun's unseeing rays.

LXIII

Against my love shall be as I am now,
With Time's injurious hand crush'd and o'erworn;
When hours have drain'd his blood and fill'd his brow
With lines and wrinkles; when his youthful morn
Hath travell'd on to age's steepy night;
And all those beauties whereof now he's king
Are vanishing, or vanished out of sight,
Stealing away the treasure of his spring;
For such a time do I now fortify
Against confounding age's cruel knife,
That he shall never cut from memory
My sweet love's beauty, though my lover's life:
  His beauty shall in these black lines be seen,
  And they shall live, and he in them still green.

63
Rachel Barnett-Jones

Old man;
I don't care about your lack of hair,
Your old man eyebrows,
Your lingering whiff of shed,
Your muttering,
Your obstinate, undeniable deafness.

I don't care about your falling asleep
half way through a conversation,
Or the way you shamble in your slippers
And tea-stained dressing gown
Through a lazy, sleepy weekend,
Or the bits of last night's dinner I find in your beard.

I love you old,
as I loved you young.

LXIV

When I have seen by Time's fell hand defac'd
The rich-proud cost of outworn buried age;
When sometime lofty towers I see down-raz'd,
And brass eternal slave to mortal rage;
When I have seen the hungry ocean gain
Advantage on the kingdom of the shore,
And the firm soil win of the watery main,
Increasing store with loss, and loss with store;
When I have seen such interchange of state,
Or state itself confounded, to decay;
Ruin hath taught me thus to ruminate –
That Time will come and take my love away.
  This thought is as a death which cannot choose
  But weep to have, that which it fears to lose.

St Margaret's and the farmhouse
Di Slaney

We were never friends, you and I;
your people slavish to the soil, my
people obedient, for the most part,
to the cross. The two only met at mart,

some half-hearth, others strictly Book
not crook. And mine never took
yours seriously, not until they
raided my foundations, paid way

over the evens to that wily clerk
who flagged stones strong enough
to build your central stack. Rough
hewn? Well, yes - we both are. Dark

Red Mansfield blocks keep us propped
down the ages. Proof that God just
might have some joint plan for us,
perhaps; an end left open, unstopped,

where we still face each other east to west,
salute our long endurance, pass His test.

LXV

Since brass, nor stone, nor earth, nor boundless sea,
But sad mortality o'ersways their power,
How with this rage shall beauty hold a plea,
Whose action is no stronger than a flower?
O! how shall summer's honey breath hold out,
Against the wrackful siege of battering days,
When rocks impregnable are not so stout,
Nor gates of steel so strong but Time decays?
O fearful meditation! where, alack,
Shall Time's best jewel from Time's chest lie hid?
Or what strong hand can hold his swift foot back?
Or who his spoil of beauty can forbid?
  O! none, unless this miracle have might,
  That in black ink my love may still shine bright.

Rave On
Miles Salter

Yes, Bill, I concur. Behind each wink and kiss,
a skull waits to unmask itself and whisper
in our busy ears. But life, a flash of light and music,
shouldn't be denied; let's roar and embrace
while light still fills the world, learn a little, travel
to places that make us bigger. Let's talk, and drink,
and beam at the brief coincidence we share.

It'll be over soon enough, Bill, the sound
and fury seeming louder when the spade
cuts into the earth to mark our bed.
But let us, small and fragile birds that we are,
turn over in the sky while we can, knowing this
dizzy summer will cool soon. But so what? We're here,
damn it, swooping and singing in the sparkle of the sun.

LXVI

Tired with all these, for restful death I cry,
As to behold desert a beggar born,
And needy nothing trimm'd in jollity,
And purest faith unhappily forsworn,
And gilded honour shamefully misplac'd,
And maiden virtue rudely strumpeted,
And right perfection wrongfully disgrac'd,
And strength by limping sway disabled
And art made tongue-tied by authority,
And folly – doctor-like – controlling skill,
And simple truth miscall'd simplicity,
And captive good attending captain ill:
  Tir'd with all these, from these would I be gone,
  Save that, to die, I leave my love alone.

66
Sarah Diamond

And how can I fear death? Life frightens me far more.
When I see child poverty negating future possibility
And Idolatry TV give birth to more celebrity.
And believing what you're told means that something's being sold.
And the raises go to bankers – never nurses, teachers, carers.
And women still don't earn as much and still don't feel safe enough.
And the NHS is under threat by corporate interest.
And decency is unelectable, derided as detestable
But Donald Trump wins votes with hate in every US state.
And what we teach is how to pass instead of how to learn.
And every other thought is how much more I need to earn.
Then death would be a peaceful pause to end this ruthless game.

For you, my daughter I must remain
And for you I can sustain.

LXVII

Ah! wherefore with infection should he live,
And with his presence grace impiety,
That sin by him advantage should achieve,
And lace itself with his society?
Why should false painting imitate his cheek,
And steel dead seeming of his living hue?
Why should poor beauty indirectly seek
Roses of shadow, since his rose is true?
Why should he live, now Nature bankrupt is,
Beggar'd of blood to blush through lively veins?
For she hath no exchequer now but his,
And proud of many, lives upon his gains.
  O! him she stores, to show what wealth she had
  In days long since, before these last so bad.

You've Missed Your Stop
Jacqueline Saphra

Free on the Tube, our aspiration rag
The Evening Standard creeps with painted lies
on bodies papped and polished till you gag
for stuff you never wanted. London shines
but not for you; between the grimy pages,
beauties flash, botox blooms and skinflints riff
on gold. The city's finest, peeled and ageless,
open up, then slam the door; as if
there were a door to this bedazzled hell
where flesh comes free to dress your feather bed,
lovely, grafted stars grow fur and tassle,
futures rise and every carpet's red.
Whose life is this? Whose godforsaken plan?
Go home. Wash the newsprint from your hands.

LXVIII

Thus is his cheek the map of days outworn,
When beauty lived and died as flowers do now,
Before these bastard signs of fair were born,
Or durst inhabit on a living brow;
Before the golden tresses of the dead,
The right of sepulchres, were shorn away,
To live a second life on second head;
Ere beauty's dead fleece made another gay:
In him those holy antique hours are seen,
Without all ornament, itself and true,
Making no summer of another's green,
Robbing no old to dress his beauty new;
  And him as for a map doth Nature store,
  To show false Art what beauty was of yore.

68
Simon Scardifield

Will, come here, two things I want to show you.
(Can I call you Will? I feel like I know you).
First: we've re-written your old wooden 'O'.
It's moved very slightly but it's all done just so:
They combed through the documents, did it from scratch,
Lime plaster, whalebone, jig at the end, thatch -
Some fire regs things they couldn't not do,
But there is your theatre, Will, itself and true.
Or not. One or two touches are missing:
The corner that the scabrous whores used to piss in,
The man at the gate with the unsavoury knife,
The rats, lice, drunks, the raw stench of life.
No beggars, or shouting, or unsightly pustules,
It's more white wine, and flapjack, and kids in cagoules.
Your theatre's second life is rather more scenic.
We like to keep antique hours nice and hygienic.
Next - you're the Elvis of culture, not some Alison Moyet,
So pull on a hat or you'll be mobbed in the foyer -
And follow me through Southwark and our dizzying times
(I'll bring you up to speed in a couple of lines:
It's all about petrol and silicon chips,
Plus smaller discoveries like toasters and zips)
And look: a stall off Rye Lane in a tiny arcade
Where they sell human hair all bunched in smooth braids.
The difference: these tresses are from brows not yet dead.
(Are you Indian, no cattle? There's a cash cow on your head).
It's all black, this shorn hair, not your Elizabeth's orange,
But still we're the same. Nothing's new. Plus ça change.

LXIX

Those parts of thee that the world's eye doth view
Want nothing that the thought of hearts can mend;
All tongues – the voice of souls – give thee that due,
Uttering bare truth, even so as foes commend.
Thy outward thus with outward praise is crown'd;
But those same tongues, that give thee so thine own,
In other accents do this praise confound
By seeing farther than the eye hath shown.
They look into the beauty of thy mind,
And that in guess they measure by thy deeds;
Then – churls – their thoughts, although their eyes were kind,
To thy fair flower add the rank smell of weeds:
  But why thy odour matcheth not thy show,
  The soil is this, that thou dost common grow.

To Measure by thy Deeds
Jonathan Davidson

Difficult not to bow down to the bright light
Gilding the good-looking as they glide across
The ornamental lake, their rich feathers white
And weightless, their gains our subtle loss.
Difficult not to be force-fed the fat words
Sung from the silver bough of a sunlit tree,
A wit to un-flight or to snare small birds,
Speaking what we think we think, but sweetly.
And impossible not to nod-through decisions
Made in our names by charmingly convincing
Blond Etonians with self-sodomising visions
Of power by any means. And thus, deceiving
  Relentlessly and often, however queasy
  Forced fooling makes us feel, is easy.

LXX

That thou art blam'd shall not be thy defect,
For slander's mark was ever yet the fair;
The ornament of beauty is suspect,
A crow that flies in heaven's sweetest air.
So thou be good, slander doth but approve
Thy worth the greater being woo'd of time;
For canker vice the sweetest buds doth love,
And thou present'st a pure unstained prime.
Thou hast passed by the ambush of young days
Either not assail'd, or victor being charg'd;
Yet this thy praise cannot be so thy praise,
To tie up envy, evermore enlarg'd,
  If some suspect of ill mask'd not thy show,
  Then thou alone kingdoms of hearts shouldst owe.

Beyond Reproach
Arrianne Destiney

Prithee,why should you so advise?
I turn my ear as often in the past
from gangrene tongues and jaded eyes,
from wicked words of jealous wrath.
I have outstrode for many years
the bitter serpents at my heels,
and never taken pleasure in their tears
or dealt to them as they would deal.
Think you after such acts of grace
I should now weaken and unlearn
the walking wit of my unturning pace
and deal out vitriolic slander in my turn?
I need not your rule, nor your court;
keep your advice and unasked support!

LXXI

No longer mourn for me when I am dead
Than you shall hear the surly sullen bell
Give warning to the world that I am fled
From this vile world with vilest worms to dwell:
Nay, if you read this line, remember not
The hand that writ it, for I love you so,
That I in your sweet thoughts would be forgot,
If thinking on me then should make you woe.
O! if, – I say you look upon this verse,
When I perhaps compounded am with clay,
Do not so much as my poor name rehearse;
But let your love even with my life decay;
  Lest the wise world should look into your moan,
  And mock you with me after I am gone.

71
Henry Stead

You were unkind to leave this film about us
  tinctured   as you knew   by a love unknown
  to most   unfathomable to more   in this cheap world
  where no bell even   cares to tell
      of your echoing death

Of course I read it   I read it over and over   and now
  I see your ink white hand   so clear I can scarce call
back the deep lines of your sleeping face
  handsome in my all embracing love for all of you

Compounded with clay? I could kiss you   or hit you
  o what I would not now give to do both   again and again
    Shakespeare   Shakespeare
      even your name is a cliché
    and clichés are perfect

Let the wise world scavenge   the depths of my moan
  our love was perfect and now you are gone

LXXII

O! lest the world should task you to recite
What merit lived in me, that you should love
After my death, – dear love, forget me quite,
For you in me can nothing worthy prove;
Unless you would devise some virtuous lie,
To do more for me than mine own desert,
And hang more praise upon deceased I
Than niggard truth would willingly impart:
O! lest your true love may seem false in this
That you for love speak well of me untrue,
My name be buried where my body is,
And live no more to shame nor me nor you.
  For I am shamed by that which I bring forth,
  And so should you, to love things nothing worth.

Bastard Apocalyptic Love Eradication
Paul Helliwell

When summer rose I threw up the sun
selling a delicious range of hot and cold
refreshments dismembering me inside
my face slapping against the savagery
of clay clerics and rebel medic ethics.

The excruciating birth of intoxication
evacuated from the fiction of bridges
being anyone else's simpering breath
numb to the knuckle of sour romance
in waves of stagnant love that hurt.

Sundown's monotony penetrates you
and me intruding from another world
to this fathomless fall in love without
loving a memory of all who will ever
expire at the end; ending in nothing.

LXXIII

That time of year thou mayst in me behold
When yellow leaves, or none, or few, do hang
Upon those boughs which shake against the cold,
Bare ruin'd choirs, where late the sweet birds sang.
In me thou see'st the twilight of such day
As after sunset fadeth in the west;
Which by and by black night doth take away,
Death's second self, that seals up all in rest.
In me thou see'st the glowing of such fire,
That on the ashes of his youth doth lie,
As the death-bed, whereon it must expire,
Consum'd with that which it was nourish'd by.
  This thou perceiv'st, which makes thy love more strong,
  To love that well, which thou must leave ere long.

The Medlar
Tim O'Leary

Count down my days and ravel the seasons
from burst of leaf to light, to dark, to dust,
as blossom's fire, lit beyond all reason,
tries to belie the temple-razers' lust.
Crepuscular on me, the hold of time
grows firmer with every setting sun,
wrapping tightly the fusc of night's design
on a world of sleep where the worldless come.
No. If you must look at me that way, see
orchards fruit anew from fertile ash,
jewels on every excarnated tree
where I once grew before life burned and slashed.
    You come for one last time, in frost, to blet
    the fruit that now gives up what none forgets.

LXXIV

But be contented: when that fell arrest
Without all bail shall carry me away,
My life hath in this line some interest,
Which for memorial still with thee shall stay.
When thou reviewest this, thou dost review
The very part was consecrate to thee:
The earth can have but earth, which is his due;
My spirit is thine, the better part of me:
So then thou hast but lost the dregs of life,
The prey of worms, my body being dead;
The coward conquest of a wretch's knife,
Too base of thee to be remembered.
  The worth of that is that which it contains,
  And that is this, and this with thee remains.

earth can have but earth
Jane McCarthy Wilkinson

for Paul

A makeshift seam, of light and stranded night,
unravels down the valley wall, as usual.
The morning leaks out on the pile of streets.

I borrow, in and out, the unspent breath
you left there, ease a downy feather from
my throat. It opens, certain as a fact;

I try another, like I would do doors,
not really wanting something that complete.
High up, a breaking twig gives way and falls.

Bright seconds bursting slowly in the air
surround your body. Holes are appearing.
The apples on the tree need picking still.

I inch about; I wear your weight in words.
You were much lighter than they ever were.

LXXV

So are you to my thoughts as food to life,
Or as sweet-season'd showers are to the ground;
And for the peace of you I hold such strife
As 'twixt a miser and his wealth is found.
Now proud as an enjoyer, and anon
Doubting the filching age will steal his treasure;
Now counting best to be with you alone,
Then better'd that the world may see my pleasure:
Sometime all full with feasting on your sight,
And by and by clean starved for a look;
Possessing or pursuing no delight,
Save what is had, or must from you be took.
    Thus do I pine and surfeit day by day,
    Or gluttoning on all, or all away.

Dinner
Hitomi Yu

I binge on your love.
Starving, then gorging. Flaunting 'us',
Then retreating.

Eating.

LXXVI

Why is my verse so barren of new pride,
So far from variation or quick change?
Why with the time do I not glance aside
To new-found methods, and to compounds strange?
Why write I still all one, ever the same,
And keep invention in a noted weed,
That every word doth almost tell my name,
Showing their birth, and where they did proceed?
O! know sweet love I always write of you,
And you and love are still my argument;
So all my best is dressing old words new,
Spending again what is already spent:
    For as the sun is daily new and old,
    So is my love still telling what is told.

Writing You
Kesha Sandon

Ok. I need to reinvent my style.
Jazz it up. Fronted adverbials? – or
Maybe rhyme. Time to do an Arvon
Or try a slam night. I might need
Some one-on-one. It's been a while.

I entered 76 poetry competitions
This year. Here's to fourth place
At Trumpton-on-Sea festival. But
Look at me now… Metaphor city,
Similes coming out of my arse.

Breakthrough? Nope. Fact remains,
Every poem I write is still about you.

LXXVII

Thy glass will show thee how thy beauties wear,
Thy dial how thy precious minutes waste;
These vacant leaves thy mind's imprint will bear,
And of this book, this learning mayst thou taste.
The wrinkles which thy glass will truly show
Of mouthed graves will give thee memory;
Thou by thy dial's shady stealth mayst know
Time's thievish progress to eternity.
Look! what thy memory cannot contain,
Commit to these waste blanks, and thou shalt find
Those children nursed, deliver'd from thy brain,
To take a new acquaintance of thy mind.
  These offices, so oft as thou wilt look,
  Shall profit thee and much enrich thy book.

Shift

Jo Brandon

It is only 7 hours and 7 minutes until
I can go home.
Someone suggested sticking a scrap of paper
over the lower, right-hand corner of my screen
but there are still the easy-to-read hands
of the office clock and the twitch of my wrist-watch.
They have recently discovered that my monitor
gives off UV light, despite the fact I am deficient
in vitamin D from being in here
twenty-eight thousand and eight-hundred seconds a day.
The air conditioning makes my hair brittle,
dries out my eyes and thins my skin;
I have a scholar's stoop from failing to meet
impossible ergonomic standards.
On the desk is my predecessor's collection of cure-alls.
I threw out her lucky heather — the purple had come away
but I keep her stash of mineral powders, hydration salts,
mood mists, ocular drops, anti-bac wipes,
flavoured balms and half-rolled tubes of lotion.
In new miscellaneous folders I tap out my wishes:
parallel here-now vignettes, future-self, happy-me —
they are all more or less the same but listing them
feels like invoking a spell.
I'm leaving them for my successor to find,
I wonder if they'll seem like gibberish to her
or an extension of the list she's left behind.

LXXVIII

So oft have I invoked thee for my Muse,
And found such fair assistance in my verse
As every alien pen hath got my use
And under thee their poesy disperse.
Thine eyes, that taught the dumb on high to sing
And heavy ignorance aloft to fly,
Have added feathers to the learned's wing
And given grace a double majesty.
Yet be most proud of that which I compile,
Whose influence is thine, and born of thee:
In others' works thou dost but mend the style,
And arts with thy sweet graces graced be;
  But thou art all my art, and dost advance
  As high as learning, my rude ignorance.

To Wikipedia
Joshua Ip

So oft have I invoked thee for amusements
Comparing pre- and post- edited versions,
Though every don accrues to thee abusements
Yet seeks thee out to document perversions.
Thine search bar, slit of wonder, master stroke,
Doth gape and gush with overflowing trivia,
Hath oft been host to self-important blokes
Who multiply their markups like chlamydia.
 Yet be most proud of my final year thesis
Whose synthesis 'twas thine own synonym –
Others might feign research through bits and pieces
Of thy bibliography verbatim.
But thou art all I cite, and all I see,
Thou sight for sore eyes, for thou sourceth me.

LXXIX

Whilst I alone did call upon thy aid,
My verse alone had all thy gentle grace;
But now my gracious numbers are decay'd,
And my sick Muse doth give an other place.
I grant, sweet love, thy lovely argument
Deserves the travail of a worthier pen;
Yet what of thee thy poet doth invent
He robs thee of, and pays it thee again.
He lends thee virtue, and he stole that word
From thy behaviour; beauty doth he give,
And found it in thy cheek: he can afford
No praise to thee, but what in thee doth live.
  Then thank him not for that which he doth say,
  Since what he owes thee, thou thyself dost pay.

79

Deanna Rodger

When I sucked the slice of all purpose cloth
through the takeaway coffee cup I groaned,
Fibres soaked in caffeine and skimmed milk froth
In the south of London the price is low.

I'd sworn that something was wrong with the lid -
Couldn't believe she'd sabotage my throat
Thick skin preventing overheated sips
Her cut eye flirt smirk, how deep could she go

With him, Latte fucker – "The change is yours.
Accidents happen Dee, don't cause a fuss."
We leave to view a flat on the third floor
Spacious rooms, though not enough between us.

Deposit too high to cash buy. "We'll call"
I love you, a scalded tongue, decoupled.

LXXX

O! how I faint when I of you do write,
Knowing a better spirit doth use your name,
And in the praise thereof spends all his might,
To make me tongue-tied speaking of your fame!
But since your worth – wide as the ocean is, –
The humble as the proudest sail doth bear,
My saucy bark, inferior far to his,
On your broad main doth wilfully appear.
Your shallowest help will hold me up afloat,
Whilst he upon your soundless deep doth ride;
Or, being wrack'd, I am a worthless boat,
He of tall building, and of goodly pride:
  Then if he thrive and I be cast away,
  The worst was this, – my love was my decay.

Wide As The Ocean Is
Rachel Plummer

I love you as the North Sea loves a boat
when bearing it high up onto the shore,
or as a piece of driftwood loves to float
in with the tide to Gullane. I adore
you as the Firth of Forth adores the train,
its track, the bridge it crosses over and
the bridge's black reflection in the rain
bloated river. I love you like the land
can't help loving the coast and breaks itself
apart to let the ocean in, and like
a dizzy, new-formed cyclone loves the Gulf
Stream, like storm water loves a lightning strike.
I love you as a drowned man loves the sea;
I am the boat that begs you shipwreck me.

LXXXI

Or I shall live your epitaph to make,
Or you survive when I in earth am rotten;
From hence your memory death cannot take,
Although in me each part will be forgotten.
Your name from hence immortal life shall have,
Though I, once gone, to all the world must die:
The earth can yield me but a common grave,
When you entombed in men's eyes shall lie.
Your monument shall be my gentle verse,
Which eyes not yet created shall o'er-read;
And tongues to be, your being shall rehearse,
When all the breathers of this world are dead;
  You still shall live, – such virtue hath my pen, –
  Where breath most breathes, even in the mouths of men.

The Poet's Curse
Katy Evans-Bush

> I can think of no finer epitaph than:
> 'She gave pleasure to her contemporaries'.
> Marie Corelli

What idiot lives for the moment? Maybe just this one:
the moment when I render you immortal.
With these two words – 'immortal', 'you' – I've done it;
in worlds to come they'll talk about your beauty.
Your fame will live in unimaginable mouths,
the dream they breathe into their foetid feathers,
those breathers still unmade who'll breathe when we
are long undone. So you die first. So I die –
this moment's done. What do we get out of bed for,
if not to make sure that dead doesn't really mean DEAD?
The past was epic. And the future, too,
is where the heroes are who're breathing now.
However shit a time you think you're having,
you're lucky. I made you someone who really *lived*.

LXXXII

I grant thou wert not married to my Muse,
And therefore mayst without attaint o'erlook
The dedicated words which writers use
Of their fair subject, blessing every book.
Thou art as fair in knowledge as in hue,
Finding thy worth a limit past my praise;
And therefore art enforced to seek anew
Some fresher stamp of the time-bettering days.
And do so, love; yet when they have devis'd,
What strained touches rhetoric can lend,
Thou truly fair, wert truly sympathiz'd
In true plain words, by thy true-telling friend;
  And their gross painting might be better us'd
  Where cheeks need blood; in thee it is abus'd.

82
Emer Gillespie

The way I write's unique, it's who I am,
these words I choose choose me, or so it seems,
life's not a competition I have found,
the prize that we all win, we win for keeps

and poetry for me's a private vice –
and pleasure – and way of making sense
of everything I think or look at twice –
the writing act a peering through a lens

to understand connections previously missed.
No public acclamation is my goal,
encouragement or praise is not the gist
of what I want from you – support is not your role.

Just don't be harsh, feel 'duty bound' to say
that you've read 'better' poets along the way.

LXXXIII

I never saw that you did painting need,
And therefore to your fair no painting set;
I found, or thought I found, you did exceed
That barren tender of a poet's debt:
And therefore have I slept in your report,
That you yourself, being extant, well might show
How far a modern quill doth come too short,
Speaking of worth, what worth in you doth grow.
This silence for my sin you did impute,
Which shall be most my glory being dumb;
For I impair not beauty being mute,
When others would give life, and bring a tomb.
  There lives more life in one of your fair eyes
  Than both your poets can in praise devise.

Letter to a Young Civil Servant
Theophilus Kwek

Finally, remember that there are ways
To proffer praise without your saying so.
If silence speaks your mind, then rest your case
And let the office work out what to do.
I know that you once signed up for this post
To change the world, or at least make your mark –
And once, like you, I thought to make the most
Of what they said was such rewarding work.
These days I spend my worry at my desk,
Bring no arguments to woo the others,
For flattery makes no good policies
And this I've found: our reward is highest
    When, unharmed by every best intention,
    Best-laid plans come to their own fruition.

LXXXIV

Who is it that says most, which can say more,
Than this rich praise, – that you alone, are you?
In whose confine immured is the store
Which should example where your equal grew.
Lean penury within that pen doth dwell
That to his subject lends not some small glory;
But he that writes of you, if he can tell
That you are you, so dignifies his story,
Let him but copy what in you is writ,
Not making worse what nature made so clear,
And such a counterpart shall fame his wit,
Making his style admired every where.
  You to your beauteous blessings add a curse,
  Being fond on praise, which makes your praises worse.

84
Alexander Velky

How best could I, presented with your form,
Begin to let you know, to make you feel,
What I felt holding you – so live, so warm,
So like a loaf of bread, so like an eel?
No photograph could ever hope to tell.
No ultrasound of my own heart could hope
To mirror the experience; to swell
You to this state – your sternum couldn't cope.
Nor could you see through my short-sighted eyes;
Nor would I wish myopia on youth.
A better writer wouldn't eulogize;
A better father would just tell the truth.
Now here's yours, still dumb, debating whether
To call you pretty or call you clever.

LXXXV

My tongue-tied Muse in manners holds her still,
While comments of your praise richly compil'd,
Reserve their character with golden quill,
And precious phrase by all the Muses fil'd.
I think good thoughts, whilst others write good words,
And like unlettered clerk still cry 'Amen'
To every hymn that able spirit affords,
In polish'd form of well-refined pen.
Hearing you praised, I say ''tis so, 'tis true,'
And to the most of praise add something more;
But that is in my thought, whose love to you,
Though words come hindmost, holds his rank before.
  Then others, for the breath of words respect,
  Me for my dumb thoughts, speaking in effect.

Tongue-tied
Robbie Burton

This time is different.
He's dropping off to sleep.
Words riot through my skull
rattling my nerves and chest,
   Come on come on, let us out.

Texting won't do.
Love needs a fine-nibbed pen
for the note I'll slip inside his wallet.
He'll chance on it
in Homebase or Greggs.

I'll be at my desk
unstoppering more thoughts.
A few will get polished.
Others screwed up.

LXXXVI

Was it the proud full sail of his great verse,
Bound for the prize of all too precious you,
That did my ripe thoughts in my brain inhearse,
Making their tomb the womb wherein they grew?
Was it his spirit, by spirits taught to write,
Above a mortal pitch, that struck me dead?
No, neither he, nor his compeers by night
Giving him aid, my verse astonished.
He, nor that affable familiar ghost
Which nightly gulls him with intelligence,
As victors of my silence cannot boast;
I was not sick of any fear from thence:
  But when your countenance fill'd up his line,
  Then lacked I matter; that enfeebled mine.

A Suggestion from The Rival Poet
Robin Houghton

I see you are in pain, but no-one needs
a pair of anything, it's too much. So – let's share

his beauty. One *all too precious* blue eye
each, I'll take the right, since the plan is mine,

and you are (as you say) the lesser poet,
so you shall have what's left. Likewise his hands –

I hear your own preferences verge on sinister,
and he may stroke me all the better with

his right. Let him stand on one leg for you,
the other for me, for he is – oh! – a mean

hopper. Then the body's long lean muscles:
fillet his thighs and scythe his chest apart,

let's watch the dark life of him quiver as we
fight over and feast on his splintered heart.

LXXXVII

Farewell! thou art too dear for my possessing,
And like enough thou know'st thy estimate,
The charter of thy worth gives thee releasing;
My bonds in thee are all determinate.
For how do I hold thee but by thy granting?
And for that riches where is my deserving?
The cause of this fair gift in me is wanting,
And so my patent back again is swerving.
Thy self thou gav'st, thy own worth then not knowing,
Or me to whom thou gav'st it, else mistaking;
So thy great gift, upon misprision growing,
Comes home again, on better judgement making.
  Thus have I had thee, as a dream doth flatter,
  In sleep a king, but waking no such matter.

After the Restraining Order
Kate Venables

I could see that you would fall for me by
the way you looked at me, the way we two
just clicked. Instead of 'Hi', you, dear, wrote 'Dear'

in emails. When we met, your startled deer
look was just so sweet. Once, you let me buy
you coffee. And when I got the tattoo

with the blazing heart, you were kind, much too
kind about the typo in your name. Dear
love – the way you helped that poor passerby!

Goodbye. You're much too good for me, my dear!

LXXXVIII

When thou shalt be dispos'd to set me light,
And place my merit in the eye of scorn,
Upon thy side, against myself I'll fight,
And prove thee virtuous, though thou art forsworn.
With mine own weakness, being best acquainted,
Upon thy part I can set down a story
Of faults conceal'd, wherein I am attainted;
That thou in losing me shalt win much glory:
And I by this will be a gainer too;
For bending all my loving thoughts on thee,
The injuries that to myself I do,
Doing thee vantage, double-vantage me.
  Such is my love, to thee I so belong,
  That for thy right, myself will bear all wrong.

The Injuries I do
Sue Rose

It is for you I set the morning's dark alight,
Undaunted by a legacy of hate and scorn.
In the life I lived before, I was afraid to fight,
Hidden beneath the blacks I'd always worn;
Then I lost my virtue, and my kin, acquainted
With the truth, could not refute the story
Of my shame. I can't have my father tainted
In my name, so I'll embrace the fire of glory
For his good and pray I'll gain by this act too;
I'm still afraid, but now I'll bow to duty
So the damage to myself and others that I do
Will raise him in your sight, and redeem me.
This is an honourable death and it won't be long
Till I'm at peace for setting right with wrong.

LXXXIX

Say that thou didst forsake me for some fault,
And I will comment upon that offence:
Speak of my lameness, and I straight will halt,
Against thy reasons making no defence.
Thou canst not love disgrace me half so ill,
To set a form upon desired change,
As I'll myself disgrace; knowing thy will,
I will acquaintance strangle, and look strange;
Be absent from thy walks; and in my tongue
Thy sweet beloved name no more shall dwell,
Lest I, too much profane, should do it wrong,
And haply of our old acquaintance tell.
　For thee, against my self I'll vow debate,
　For I must ne'er love him whom thou dost hate.

Shrouds
Richy Campbell

After my finger has left the light switch
The blame, once more, shrouds the room with the black
Turns red, spider-webbed, after close of eyes.
A small forever, then I fall asleep.

I dream of forefingers that point and float
The worst of my flaws read loud in my voice;
I dream of a photo being drained of colour
Till a white card's left, a rainbow trickles.

Next morning, back propped against the head-board
I fixate on the sight of the future:
My town, halved, since I bricked the streets we shared
My tongue, dumb, since I banned your syllables.

I lift my chin, the sight I catch still sore
Six perfect paint-squares, on a sun-bleached wall.

XC

Then hate me when thou wilt; if ever, now;
Now, while the world is bent my deeds to cross,
Join with the spite of fortune, make me bow,
And do not drop in for an after-loss:
Ah! do not, when my heart hath 'scap'd this sorrow,
Come in the rearward of a conquer'd woe;
Give not a windy night a rainy morrow,
To linger out a purpos'd overthrow.
If thou wilt leave me, do not leave me last,
When other petty griefs have done their spite,
But in the onset come: so shall I taste
At first the very worst of fortune's might;
   And other strains of woe, which now seem woe,
   Compar'd with loss of thee, will not seem so.

90
Pooja Nansi

The morning that I must learn to leave you
there will be lilies wilting in the
vase, there will be one dozen eggs
that will never make it to
breakfast. Love, this isn't
devastation. It's
how loss begins
the minute
we are
born.
It's how
we learn to
lose the exact
moment we learn how
to love. See how unarmed
we are against life's many
earthquakes, how vulnerable, how
freed. Everything is stretching toward
an end, even the bravest, fiercest seed.

XCI

Some glory in their birth, some in their skill,
Some in their wealth, some in their body's force,
Some in their garments though new-fangled ill;
Some in their hawks and hounds, some in their horse;
And every humour hath his adjunct pleasure,
Wherein it finds a joy above the rest:
But these particulars are not my measure,
All these I better in one general best.
Thy love is better than high birth to me,
Richer than wealth, prouder than garments' costs,
Of more delight than hawks and horses be;
And having thee, of all men's pride I boast:
  Wretched in this alone, that thou mayst take
  All this away, and me most wretchcd make.

The Language we Cry in
Nick Makoha

Famine, the first sorrow moves like an unseen breath.
I waste my temper looking at a hole in the sky.
Mystics lead the rich, hardwired for magic to their death.
The villain lit by a crescent moon hangs my alibi
by a power cord in a cane field to fulfil the prophecy,
surrounded by sentinels, lessor gods, and jackals
howling at the hills. Idle vehicles full of appetite pant in these
last days of the old world. My feet are soaked in diesel,
its body's members wish they were water in a new glass.
The night mends itself as the shape of me fumbles a confession.
My visible reflection in a gazelle's eye as clouds pass.
In this last scene the names I carry are printed on a television.
Of all the lies people tell themselves rumours are language of war.
Kinsmen will deny they know my broken body resting by the shore.

XCII

But do thy worst to steal thyself away,
For term of life thou art assured mine;
And life no longer than thy love will stay,
For it depends upon that love of thine.
Then need I not to fear the worst of wrongs,
When in the least of them my life hath end.
I see a better state to me belongs
Than that which on thy humour doth depend:
Thou canst not vex me with inconstant mind,
Since that my life on thy revolt doth lie.
O! what a happy title do I find,
Happy to have thy love, happy to die!
  But what's so blessed-fair that fears no blot?
  Thou mayst be false, and yet I know it not.

I have never dreaded you leaving, since
Mary Jean Chan

Our terrors are not Shakespeare's. Lovers with
the same anatomies, our bodies made
in one another's likeness. Us circling

this city, asking whether we could live
as if we were not his or her mistake,
if we could love as if another's breath

were blessing, could write blasphemy on bare
flesh. The year I was born, 1990 –
the WHO declassified homo-

sexuality as mental illness.
The night we met, we walked along a street
drenched in tears. Above us the moon. All this

time I wondered what lines were being crossed –
a bouquet of fingers blooming between
us – an act so public that shame becomes

private. Our dangers are not Shakespeare's: Death,
Revolt. Mine was surrendering, at last,
to desire – you hovering above me

like a knife-blade, my palm on a foreign
pulse. This bridge of sighs, our hands light as light
on skin. This note of your being – a clef

humming with need. We bleed dark between our
legs, mastering the tune and texture of
push-pull, of touch. Our joys are not Shakespeare's.

Now I imbibe your scent to keep the world's
wounds at bay, your torso a tapestry
cued in by moonlight, pinning me to ground.

XCIII

So shall I live, supposing thou art true,
Like a deceived husband; so love's face
May still seem love to me, though alter'd new;
Thy looks with me, thy heart in other place:
For there can live no hatred in thine eye,
Therefore in that I cannot know thy change.
In many's looks, the false heart's history
Is writ in moods, and frowns, and wrinkles strange.
But heaven in thy creation did decree
That in thy face sweet love should ever dwell;
Whate'er thy thoughts, or thy heart's workings be,
Thy looks should nothing thence, but sweetness tell.
　How like Eve's apple doth thy beauty grow,
　If thy sweet virtue answer not thy show!

His Lover, on Reading Sonnet 93
David Clarke

What is it, love, you think I do not show?
You try me with your questioning. I grow
a little stranger to you. What's to tell
that looks and touch conceal? Should I then be
transparent like a doll of glass, to dwell
among physicians' specimens? Decree
me faker, hypocrite. Is it not strange
to kiss a liar and trash our history?
Absurd, my dear, when you're the one to change
and change the whole world in your jealous eye.
Years hence, you'll glimpse me in some other place,
when once again I've made my life anew –
will you have learned by then to read a face
that's learned at last to blankly be untrue?

XCIV

They that have power to hurt, and will do none,
That do not do the thing they most do show,
Who, moving others, are themselves as stone,
Unmoved, cold, and to temptation slow;
They rightly do inherit heaven's graces,
And husband nature's riches from expense;
They are the lords and owners of their faces,
Others, but stewards of their excellence.
The summer's flower is to the summer sweet,
Though to itself, it only live and die,
But if that flower with base infection meet,
The basest weed outbraves his dignity:
  For sweetest things turn sourest by their deeds;
  Lilies that fester, smell far worse than weeds.

photographer
Mandy Sutter

when with student eyes   we
wrote you off   sagging
jeans   flaccid fleece   not
a talker   head down walker
whose glasses   rode
a greasy nose   we didn't spot
your cool gaze   days on foot
grass and twigs   you lit to cook
nor saw you doze   and wake
in a bag   to bring us that dawn
pine   mirrored   in a brass lake
then we knew   you had ten
thousand ways to say one thing
the world is holy   look

XCV

How sweet and lovely dost thou make the shame
Which, like a canker in the fragrant rose,
Doth spot the beauty of thy budding name!
O! in what sweets dost thou thy sins enclose.
That tongue that tells the story of thy days,
Making lascivious comments on thy sport,
Cannot dispraise, but in a kind of praise;
Naming thy name, blesses an ill report.
O! what a mansion have those vices got
Which for their habitation chose out thee,
Where beauty's veil doth cover every blot
And all things turns to fair that eyes can see!
  Take heed, dear heart, of this large privilege;
  The hardest knife ill-us'd doth lose his edge.

Skull Threshold
Hilary Watson

The bear caught inside the trap –
ragged raw against the metal,

you clear the ground around the bolted box,
rip up brambles, avoid making eyes.

Settle sticks for rooms around him. Batter boards,
slab floors, fell trees for corner stakes. Rat sills.

Gather straw, fix shit, mix flour, newsprint.
Let the building spread her legs

across the arid concrete.
Electrics, gas, sewage pipes,

stairways, floorboards.
Roofed and insulated, the scaffolds

folded down. *For Sale* sign.
Stravinsky's *Rite of Spring*

jostling through the passages.
The cellar stacked with last summer's

blackberry wine, bottles bloated
under the forest floor. The rafters

holding up the house
like protracted claws.

XCVI

Some say thy fault is youth, some wantonness;
Some say thy grace is youth and gentle sport;
Both grace and faults are lov'd of more and less:
Thou mak'st faults graces that to thee resort.
As on the finger of a throned queen
The basest jewel will be well esteem'd,
So are those errors that in thee are seen
To truths translated, and for true things deem'd.
How many lambs might the stern wolf betray,
If like a lamb he could his looks translate!
How many gazers mightst thou lead away,
if thou wouldst use the strength of all thy state!
  But do not so; I love thee in such sort,
  As, thou being mine, mine is thy good report.

Accounting for You
William Doreski

Neither reporting it on paper
nor engraving it in marble,
but quick as a pistol shot
I zap across the Atlantic
my digital account of you.
Everyone has heard of you,
all tourists in the sublime.
They admire your lavish acts
critiquing the physical world
and rescuing lust from despair.
They gladly honor your effort,
although it's only a gesture
flailing in yellow spring rain.
My report translates your flesh
and bone into something eager
and abstract as swallows in flight.
Whoever reads it will thrill
to embrace this shadow: all
that lingers when the fear fades
and daffodils nod in the light.

XCVII

How like a winter hath my absence been
From thee, the pleasure of the fleeting year!
What freezings have I felt, what dark days seen!
What old December's bareness everywhere!
And yet this time removed was summer's time;
The teeming autumn, big with rich increase,
Bearing the wanton burden of the prime,
Like widow'd wombs after their lords' decease:
Yet this abundant issue seem'd to me
But hope of orphans, and unfather'd fruit;
For summer and his pleasures wait on thee,
And, thou away, the very birds are mute:
  Or, if they sing, 'tis with so dull a cheer,
  That leaves look pale, dreading the winter's near.

A Response to Sonnet 97, wherein Will Shakespeare is so distraught at the loss of his son Hamnet, he finds himself writing a Petrarchan sonnet
Aileen La Tourette

Everything sucks, as Shakespeare might have said,
– don't talk to me about your daffodils,
Will, I'll take gentle grey pussy willows
that hold our names and better rest our dead –
yes, I know you, and everything you said.
I know all writers, every syllable
whirls me like Francesca but I billow
through space alone, with voices in my head.
Seasons are gone now, seasons that spice time
as seasoning does food. What's left is freeze,
where salt loses its savour and the sky its blue.
I lose my sense of Shakespeare and his rhymes,
– my sonnet is by Petrarch, not by me.
Petrarch, you knew. You lost a child, too.

XCVIII

From you have I been absent in the spring,
When proud-pied April, dress'd in all his trim,
Hath put a spirit of youth in every thing,
That heavy Saturn laugh'd and leap'd with him.
Yet nor the lays of birds, nor the sweet smell
Of different flowers in odour and in hue,
Could make me any summer's story tell,
Or from their proud lap pluck them where they grew:
Nor did I wonder at the lily's white,
Nor praise the deep vermilion in the rose;
They were but sweet, but figures of delight,
Drawn after you, you pattern of all those.
  Yet seem'd it winter still, and you away,
  As with your shadow I with these did play.

98: Plumber's Mate
Geraldine Clarkson

Dumb you, you gave consent for that first fling
(damn you, for my assent to that First Thing).

Deadheaded spring, spring-headed Daddy,
spring-loaded, proud-piped king
with all the trimmings, zinging —

decades of me anonymous in odour, hue,
punctilious free-loader you, plucking men
from my lap — conduit, sump —

You could tell any spanner's story.
My terror of paper's white, tender
but unbounded; period blood; blue
choler. Palimpsest of you,

Father. First frost closed me off, lagging
baby, airlocked teen, stopcock, premature
cadaver, shadow of you, the original
blue choler worker.

XCIX

The forward violet thus did I chide:
Sweet thief, whence didst thou steal thy sweet that smells,
If not from my love's breath? The purple pride
Which on thy soft cheek for complexion dwells
In my love's veins thou hast too grossly dy'd.
The lily I condemned for thy hand,
And buds of marjoram had stol'n thy hair;
The roses fearfully on thorns did stand,
One blushing shame, another white despair;
A third, nor red nor white, had stol'n of both,
And to his robbery had annex'd thy breath;
But, for his theft, in pride of all his growth
A vengeful canker eat him up to death.
  More flowers I noted, yet I none could see,
  But sweet, or colour it had stol'n from thee.

Flowers
Charlie May

I've always like my flowers bright.
Riots of bluebells in a Devon hedge.
Daffodils proclaiming the spring.
Roses bursting with unconfessed possibility
And the fragile lily, drooping on her
Kitchen table.

My mother was the flowers she tended.
Stooping in the garden, to love
Each splash of colour, each scent
That took her away from the fugged-up
Fumes of this place he had brought
Her too.

Nothing hurt more than the neat,
Constrained bouquets sent to bid her
Farewell. I longed to untie them all
And scatter them on her coffin. Or simply
Guild it with a daisy chain.
She is somewhere now, pruning a
Rhodedendron.

C

Where art thou Muse that thou forget'st so long,
To speak of that which gives thee all thy might?
Spend'st thou thy fury on some worthless song,
Darkening thy power to lend base subjects light?
Return forgetful Muse, and straight redeem,
In gentle numbers time so idly spent;
Sing to the ear that doth thy lays esteem
And gives thy pen both skill and argument.
Rise, resty Muse, my love's sweet face survey,
If Time have any wrinkle graven there;
If any, be a satire to decay,
And make time's spoils despised every where.
  Give my love fame faster than Time wastes life,
  So thou prevent'st his scythe and crooked knife.

Mirror, Mirror
Mark Huband

Our words are silent now, if truth be told,
since what became of us became a past
we hoped with each soft new breath we might hold
as words, in hands whose grip no time outlasts.
You are never – the never that never
would be gone nor old nor disappeared
into midnight's hollow. The believer
we together bore, became the feared
passage into age. Will we speak again,
when morning's silence passes into dreams
of that eternity we shaped in vain?
Our words are silent now, or so it seems,
 as we look into the glass of what once
 was a sacred world where the sun would dance.

CI

O truant Muse what shall be thy amends
For thy neglect of truth in beauty dy'd?
Both truth and beauty on my love depends;
So dost thou too, and therein dignified.
Make answer Muse: wilt thou not haply say,
'Truth needs no colour, with his colour fix'd;
Beauty no pencil, beauty's truth to lay;
But best is best, if never intermix'd'?
Because he needs no praise, wilt thou be dumb?
Excuse not silence so, for't lies in thee
To make him much outlive a gilded tomb
And to be prais'd of ages yet to be.
  Then do thy office, Muse; I teach thee how
  To make him seem long hence as he shows now.

101
Helena Johnson

Perhaps some things are better left, forgotten;
the photos, with our flowers fresh as spring,
and smiling, like we'll never know them rotten,
or rings, or arms, encircling nothing.
A monument to love is still a tomb,
however many visitors it draws
to honour how it once lit up a room;
the vital stuff's oblivious, outdoors.
I made a solemn promise to myself,
to never jot a word upon his name;
he would not find his carcass on the shelf,
or trace a line of sadness, or of blame.
I'd leave the sorry death in one-oh-one,
and shut my heart upon it, and be done.

CII

My love is strengthen'd, though more weak in seeming;
I love not less, though less the show appear;
That love is merchandiz'd, whose rich esteeming,
The owner's tongue doth publish every where.
Our love was new, and then but in the spring,
When I was wont to greet it with my lays;
As Philomel in summer's front doth sing,
And stops her pipe in growth of riper days:
Not that the summer is less pleasant now
Than when her mournful hymns did hush the night,
But that wild music burthens every bough,
And sweets grown common lose their dear delight.
  Therefore like her, I sometime hold my tongue:
  Because I would not dull you with my song.

The Survivor
Van Badham

Morning sunbeam illuminates cream sheets,
pale pillows. Above, a window shows her
sky without clouds. Her lover is awake;
but when she touches him, he rolls away.

It's spring outside. A year since they first kissed.
As strangers, in this bed, he fucked her wet, hot,
grabbed at her unknown limbs with frantic hands.
She burned to learn his secrets; now, she knows

this morning's cold division of their bed
grew with the size of love between them.
It's shaped like a childhood violence, the scar
of which he's only ever shown to her.

Silence speaks of how he's severed.
She'll endure. Love's forever.

CIII

Alack! what poverty my Muse brings forth,
That having such a scope to show her pride,
The argument, all bare, is of more worth
Than when it hath my added praise beside!
O! blame me not, if I no more can write!
Look in your glass, and there appears a face
That over-goes my blunt invention quite,
Dulling my lines, and doing me disgrace.
Were it not sinful then, striving to mend,
To mar the subject that before was well?
For to no other pass my verses tend
Than of your graces and your gifts to tell;
  And more, much more, than in my verse can sit,
  Your own glass shows you when you look in it.

Portrait Painting
Hamid Khanbhai

The window's high, diffuse and simplifying light
articulates the playful rhythms in your face,
which rearrange, with every turn or subtle list;
and now the hair about your ear is out of place,

inspiring me to take a fresh direction,
grasp a different form, a new idea
of you, until I'm chasing shadow shapes
around a canvas map that won't come clear.

No matter: the act of sitting there in silence,
yielding all the contours of your lips and nose
to observation, an omnivorous look,

lets slip at times an unexpected essence –
a moue that only the bathroom mirror knows;
that slung-back, seal-honk laugh when you unhook.

CIV

To me, fair friend, you never can be old,
For as you were when first your eye I ey'd,
Such seems your beauty still. Three winters cold,
Have from the forests shook three summers' pride,
Three beauteous springs to yellow autumn turn'd,
In process of the seasons have I seen,
Three April perfumes in three hot Junes burn'd,
Since first I saw you fresh, which yet are green.
Ah! yet doth beauty like a dial-hand,
Steal from his figure, and no pace perceiv'd;
So your sweet hue, which methinks still doth stand,
Hath motion, and mine eye may be deceiv'd:
  For fear of which, hear this thou age unbred:
  Ere you were born was beauty's summer dead.

Jubilate For My Fair Friend
after Shakespeare's sonnet 104 and Christopher Smart
David Attwooll

For like a cat you explore the point to the next beach, and the one after that
For your ankles dancing under Greek stars
For you make the waves in my spacetime, lighten gravity
For inviting me to that party in '72, and for the forty-three years since
For Duke St., Birch St., and Sq. Gardette
For you live in a generous time zone
For you are generous with others, and curious about their lives
For you read their stories on cards in shop windows and on gravestones
For your ammortizzatori posteriori
For your delicate sneezes that count odd numbers
For your default tune is 'The Frog Song'
For three lovely babies, and the differences between them
For the pottery jug fetish and your spotty socks
For the flying unbrushed hair at the back of your head
For the nape of your neck and the small pulse in the crook of your arm
For you trace an atlas of remembered places on my back while you read
For your secret middle name
For your smile
For the life of my love

CV

Let not my love be call'd idolatry,
Nor my beloved as an idol show,
Since all alike my songs and praises be
To one, of one, still such, and ever so.
Kind is my love to-day, to-morrow kind,
Still constant in a wondrous excellence;
Therefore my verse to constancy confin'd,
One thing expressing, leaves out difference.
'Fair, kind, and true,' is all my argument,
'Fair, kind, and true,' varying to other words;
And in this change is my invention spent,
Three themes in one, which wondrous scope affords.
  Fair, kind, and true, have often liv'd alone,
  Which three till now, never kept seat in one.

Idols
James Peake

A single earphone
in case I'm followed
and someone watches me, waiting,
not breaking the tension
of known and unknown,
watching the coat and dress
in which I am a shape,
a repertoire of shapes
and what they tell him about my flesh
(I'll gauge his eyes or worse)
and I walk hard and fast
and bring up your profile,
your face aglow in my hand,
my pocket, I almost feel it,
and uneventful distance
brings confidence,
I breathe through my mouth,
let my listening return
to the superstar dead men
in my remaining earphone.

CVI

When in the chronicle of wasted time
I see descriptions of the fairest wights,
And beauty making beautiful old rime,
In praise of ladies dead and lovely knights,
Then, in the blazon of sweet beauty's best,
Of hand, of foot, of lip, of eye, of brow,
I see their antique pen would have express'd
Even such a beauty as you master now.
So all their praises are but prophecies
Of this our time, all you prefiguring;
And for they looked but with divining eyes,
They had not skill enough your worth to sing:
  For we, which now behold these present days,
  Have eyes to wonder, but lack tongues to praise.

Vintage
Penny Boxall

Any given morning always yields
fresh binbagged batches slumping on the stoop,
the discarded, uncollected, the unwanted
present. This is where years gather
when they're through.

Careless libraries unfold
from holdalls dumped in treasuries of dust.
Ancient novels; thrillers where the plot's worn
through; cookbooks edited with gravy stains.
Slim collections rack up miles by inches.
They won't take video now, the spooling film
too big a risk, too quick to take the bait
of wayward heat. They're worried it might catch.

And then the garments... Workers sift for gold,
firing steam like guns to blast what's gone
before, but they can't cancel it all out:
a well-forgotten spritz of perfume clings
like a soul. It's hung tight in this material
for fifty years.
You force into the old
style, hold your breath, turn to the deadened light.
Look, this seam and dart, this line – there's something
you've been looking for, that thing you love.
The pattern's lost. It fits you like a glove.

CVII

Not mine own fears, nor the prophetic soul
Of the wide world dreaming on things to come,
Can yet the lease of my true love control,
Supposed as forfeit to a confin'd doom.
The mortal moon hath her eclipse endur'd,
And the sad augurs mock their own presage;
Incertainties now crown themselves assur'd,
And peace proclaims olives of endless age.
Now with the drops of this most balmy time,
My love looks fresh, and Death to me subscribes,
Since, spite of him, I'll live in this poor rime,
While he insults o'er dull and speechless tribes:
  And thou in this shalt find thy monument,
  When tyrants' crests and tombs of brass are spent.

this depics the sad moment when you realise your beatuiful relation hip clearly hasnt workt out
(an anagram of shaxespeares 107st sonnet)
leoemercer

<<!!!The start reminds me ofan_awellauncthee
cos rts so like kuic,.epic,.super;natuoral,:
>Sayhello to life!< Ee a new match, neew leuel:)
Is thsi here loue?Arcitipal creation? Pureus?
Did th efutire iust_escblode or ssometthinw??
eec_Im readie to ipgrade me to seconndd life..>
Rsnt it strandche , now timeso short
id bye it awaie for u mh?h fhpsr Asshole<!u infesteedc
ondom
Iusturn offthe mrcrophone fsnrsm Hoos gutting
onions> Enpty bedso binge thy diet fleschlease
_Door Monsoon Semenmm :Be eros ona ghost outing
alone in sodom ,Rs thrs waht deaths feels lice:<
lol Hoo needs a trmmpet., my tears mache sound:
Whateer happens, we happend. Un-us.done "Us>>

CVIII

What's in the brain, that ink may character,
Which hath not figur'd to thee my true spirit?
What's new to speak, what now to register,
That may express my love, or thy dear merit?
Nothing, sweet boy; but yet, like prayers divine,
I must each day say o'er the very same;
Counting no old thing old, thou mine, I thine,
Even as when first I hallow'd thy fair name.
So that eternal love in love's fresh case,
Weighs not the dust and injury of age,
Nor gives to necessary wrinkles place,
But makes antiquity for aye his page;
  Finding the first conceit of love there bred,
  Where time and outward form would show it dead.

108
Rebecca Russell

I'd lived a whole life before you
And questioned if I deserved another
To rewrite, to change direction
Or make do with only half a life,
Half of me wasted?
Or, half of me saved, redeemed, made whole?
Embryonic light
Too far away to yet dream of even weaning
And watching, waiting,
Not knowing that this was preordered,
Preordained by those same stars.
Waiting for you to come to your senses
Not knowing you already had
And now, lifetimes later
In landscapes imagined ancient
Eyes immortal see love, still new.
I need you to know
Definitely, absolutely know
And the world will know
Now, bearing witness, because
My words will never die, nor ever fade,
Indelible in the mind of man
And when they are said, wherever they are said,
They will always be said to you
Whether by actor or poet or parent or congregation
My words
I love you.
You.

CIX

O! never say that I was false of heart,
Though absence seem'd my flame to qualify,
As easy might I from my self depart
As from my soul which in thy breast doth lie:
That is my home of love: if I have rang'd,
Like him that travels, I return again;
Just to the time, not with the time exchang'd,
So that myself bring water for my stain.
Never believe though in my nature reign'd,
All frailties that besiege all kinds of blood,
That it could so preposterously be stain'd,
To leave for nothing all thy sum of good;
  For nothing this wide universe I call,
  Save thou, my rose, in it thou art my all.

109
Ann Kelley

Oh!
It happens –
you are faithless, false, and forgiven
once, twice if you are lucky
and I let you back,
but the heart hurts, bleeds, breaks,
and if you ever do it again
forgiveness is out of the question.
Love leaves – you kicked it out.
So forget it, don't plead.
Go!

CX

Alas! 'tis true, I have gone here and there,
And made my self a motley to the view,
Gor'd mine own thoughts, sold cheap what is most dear,
Made old offences of affections new;
Most true it is, that I have look'd on truth
Askance and strangely; but, by all above,
These blenches gave my heart another youth,
And worse essays prov'd thee my best of love.
Now all is done, save what shall have no end:
Mine appetite I never more will grind
On newer proof, to try an older friend,
A god in love, to whom I am confin'd.
  Then give me welcome, next my heaven the best,
  Even to thy pure and most most loving breast.

110
Gus Simonovic

Alas, it's true, you have gone here and there.
Hear now: my heart is open and your pronouncement
of a return, your sworn presence, does make it pulse a
little faster.
At the same time, look!
Look at my heart as it were a landscape, the shoreline of
an island. The very breast that welcomes you, you as a
wave. The one next to heaven. The heaven you think
you know.

For the sands, your grand, self-proclaimed –
homecoming-splash is as big as any.
Your song of apologia, your idolatrous cry – makes you
no more, or less, welcome.
This foreshore was chosen by you; as you were, as you
are, and as you are going to be.

I did miss your surf, all those crashes on the other
shores, chasing sailing boats,
swerving in the middle of the ocean. Your wish for no-
end-love is granted;
so long as you can endure the sounds and swashes, the
ones you couldn't notice while away – cheering my
heart, wetting my shorelines... the old froth, and the
new swell.

A breast can miss one throb, the shore can reject a
foolish wave
But... no ripple owns a private beach, as no heart
repeats the same beat.

CXI

O! for my sake do you with Fortune chide,
The guilty goddess of my harmful deeds,
That did not better for my life provide
Than public means which public manners breeds.
Thence comes it that my name receives a brand,
And almost thence my nature is subdu'd
To what it works in, like the dyer's hand:
Pity me, then, and wish I were renew'd;
Whilst, like a willing patient, I will drink,
Potions of eisel 'gainst my strong infection;
No bitterness that I will bitter think,
Nor double penance, to correct correction.
  Pity me then, dear friend, and I assure ye,
  Even that your pity is enough to cure me.

At the Globe
James Penn

Here, by the Thames, on Bankside, in Southwark
No more than two hundred metres (I'm told)
From where the original once stood, I enter
The artful anachronism of the Globe;
And fill the pit with groundlings, stalls
With merchants, boxes with nobles, conspicuous
And confident, centred round themselves, the cast
Preparing themselves in the tiring house,
Laughing, and gaze at you our guide.
Worth writing a poem about, and young
Enough to be unmarried, I'd say.

And immediately, transported in time, through
The wooden 'O' of the imagination, I move
To London, leave the wife behind in the Midlands
('Stratford to be precise, small, two hundred people, you
Wouldn't notice it if passing in your coach'),
The children cared for by the in-laws,
Conveniently incommunicado, while I
Freed from such encumbrances, could grind
My wits on Elizabethan glass, cultivate the friendship
Entirely of non-provincial people, exchange
Experiences of past loves with peers, and keep
Someone like you as a companion, a wife-in-waiting,
Courtesan, ensconced in some attic room in the building
That only Kemp or Burbage knew about, the sounds
Of London streaming through the lattice holes,
While outside an endless stream of Puritans
Would pass in disapproval, each one trying
Unsuccessfully to set fire to the straw roof.

CXII

Your love and pity doth the impression fill,
Which vulgar scandal stamp'd upon my brow;
For what care I who calls me well or ill,
So you o'er-green my bad, my good allow?
You are my all-the-world, and I must strive
To know my shames and praises from your tongue;
None else to me, nor I to none alive,
That my steel'd sense or changes right or wrong.
In so profound abysm I throw all care
Of others' voices, that my adder's sense
To critic and to flatterer stopped are.
Mark how with my neglect I do dispense:
  You are so strongly in my purpose bred,
  That all the world besides methinks are dead.

112
Shomit Dutta

Let's live and love, and count
the whole world's frown as nil;
better still, absorb its slurs
as spurs to brinkmanship,
outface it brazen hordes
and race them gaily toward
the cliff's edge.

Where you comprise my world
in one, their numbers come
to nothing, none. If they
sling mud at us, we'll kick
dust in their eyes; besides,
we'll stamp a frantic dance
on lumpen soil, and lance
the world's boil.

CXIII

Since I left you, mine eye is in my mind;
And that which governs me to go about
Doth part his function and is partly blind,
Seems seeing, but effectually is out;
For it no form delivers to the heart
Of bird, of flower, or shape which it doth latch:
Of his quick objects hath the mind no part,
Nor his own vision holds what it doth catch;
For if it see the rud'st or gentlest sight,
The most sweet favour or deformed'st creature,
The mountain or the sea, the day or night:
The crow, or dove, it shapes them to your feature.
  Incapable of more, replete with you,
  My most true mind thus maketh mine untrue.

The Crow and the Dove Take Your Shape
Anna Kisby

You leave behind a note on your Facebook wall. Your posts halt.
That's how I find out you are gone.

I try to walk you out of mind but the lane
from my cottage is a bridge to Brooklyn. Bare networks
of winter trees are steel struts from which a man once fell.
The jackdaw in the cedar eyeballs me, wears your flat-top.
The stile's stubbled wood, hand in my hand.

I try to walk you out of mind but birds are sirens
rising from ferns at my footfall. In the abandoned dovecote
your every white shirt is neatly folded. Clouds over Chalk Hill
are laundered sheets in that Manhattan hotel – threadbare,
memory worn thin in places.

A caw inside my brain, a wing-beat pulse.
The crow who foretells rain. After rain, the homecoming dove.

CXIV

Or whether doth my mind, being crown'd with you,
Drink up the monarch's plague, this flattery?
Or whether shall I say, mine eye saith true,
And that your love taught it this alchemy,
To make of monsters and things indigest
Such cherubins as your sweet self resemble,
Creating every bad a perfect best,
As fast as objects to his beams assemble?
O! 'tis the first, 'tis flattery in my seeing,
And my great mind most kingly drinks it up:
Mine eye well knows what with his gust is 'greeing,
And to his palate doth prepare the cup:
　If it be poison'd, 'tis the lesser sin
　That mine eye loves it and doth first begin.

Case Study: Sonnet 114
for Bill Shaxberd
Amy Neilson Smith

Cracking the dichotomy of the case was the study's main aim – the reliance of the eye to the mind, and the mind to the eye. The intrinsic developmental thinking into the dupery of the ego. Medical experts claimed the absence of his skull (400 years after his death) made further investigations near impossible to carry out. Indeed, the total absence of the brain made neurological excavation obsolete. Psychologists told them to read into the meaning of the poem; offered them Freud. Medical experts then exclaimed: *computer says no!* Biologists discussed cranium measurements with archivists over dinner; archivists more inclined to quill-etched topography than tape measures. Needless to say, there were no second dates. Archeologists found the subject's (aka Bill's) rapier still intact; there was no evidence to suggest that it had been touched by the youth in Sonnet 114; nor was there evidence to suggest that it hadn't. No-one knew if the falsetto-toned doe had asked to hold this bold falchion in hand: to feel the smoothness of its adamantine spear, to joust – oscillating through flesh, to dance for this prince of parchment, to toe the line of a lutetium-laced moment – tease a catalyst till it almost breaks, to secure his place at the royal dinner table, to set his beating jewel in his liege's chest. To feed. There is no hard or fast evidence to suggest any of this. (Please see archeological records for further information: www.billsrapier.com). The investigation of dichotomy remained inconclusive; neither exhaustive – everything belonging to one part or the other (attached), or mutually exclusive – nothing belonging simultaneously to both parts (detached): the logistics of love. Centuries later, readers still peruse the poem with interest.

CXV

Those lines that I before have writ do lie,
Even those that said I could not love you dearer:
Yet then my judgment knew no reason why
My most full flame should afterwards burn clearer.
But reckoning Time, whose million'd accidents
Creep in 'twixt vows, and change decrees of kings,
Tan sacred beauty, blunt the sharp'st intents,
Divert strong minds to the course of altering things;
Alas! why fearing of Time's tyranny,
Might I not then say, 'Now I love you best,'
When I was certain o'er incertainty,
Crowning the present, doubting of the rest?
  Love is a babe, then might I not say so,
  To give full growth to that which still doth grow?

115
Simon Barraclough

Those wars that I before have waged do lie,
Even those that said I could not kill you better,
Yet then my gen'rals knew no reason why
My most fierce flame should afterwards burn hotter.

But reckoning time, whose million'd barrel bombs
Bounce in 'twixt vows and change decrees of kings,
Annih'late beauty, char lithe bodies into tombs,
Flay the tender skin to which sweet agony clings;

Alas, why, fearing of time's tyranny,
Might I not then say, 'Now I hate you best',
When I was certain o'er uncertainty,
And could've fucked you into rape, incest;
War's all the rage, then might I not say so,
To give full growth to wroth which still doth grow?

CXVI

Let me not to the marriage of true minds
Admit impediments. Love is not love
Which alters when it alteration finds,
Or bends with the remover to remove:
O, no! it is an ever-fixed mark,
That looks on tempests and is never shaken;
It is the star to every wandering bark,
Whose worth's unknown, although his height be taken.
Love's not Time's fool, though rosy lips and cheeks
Within his bending sickle's compass come;
Love alters not with his brief hours and weeks,
But bears it out even to the edge of doom.
  If this be error and upon me prov'd,
  I never writ, nor no man ever lov'd.

Hiss
Stav Poleg

Where has she gone? Lights! Camera! A carousel
moon! The sky is dark with astronomy. The city, a pivoting
needle, a compass stone-thrown from the shore.
Somewhere a star is unfixed from a roof, a blue slate
falls to the ground. Ladies and Gentlemen, I give you the fool
who drinks herself sober by the pier's falling light.
The rain has shaken itself with wild winter. The city has sunset
into the water like a glass-vessel star. Love
hours and tempests in the flickering night. The river shoots smoke
from boathouses, smoke separates into magnetic-north
fog. Take 1. Prosecco, the colour of rose.
Take 2. The girl shouts to the 4 a.m. street: *Here is my star*
for your every lost ship. Take 3. She knocks on the ever-fixed hiss
of a door. Her shout, a black iris, steering the street to the core.

CXVII

Accuse me thus: that I have scanted all,
Wherein I should your great deserts repay,
Forgot upon your dearest love to call,
Whereto all bonds do tie me day by day;
That I have frequent been with unknown minds,
And given to time your own dear-purchas'd right;
That I have hoisted sail to all the winds
Which should transport me farthest from your sight.
Book both my wilfulness and errors down,
And on just proof surmise, accumulate;
Bring me within the level of your frown,
But shoot not at me in your waken'd hate;
  Since my appeal says I did strive to prove
  The constancy and virtue of your love.

Catalogue
MD Anson

He'd made a list.
A catalogue of my domestic misdemeanours.
He thought it would give a structure to our conversation.

It gave a structure:
A pathway to the clouds, looping out the window
Into the night. It was time for stars. For wind. For flight.

CXVIII

Like as, to make our appetite more keen,
With eager compounds we our palate urge;
As, to prevent our maladies unseen,
We sicken to shun sickness when we purge;
Even so, being full of your ne'er-cloying sweetness,
To bitter sauces did I frame my feeding;
And, sick of welfare, found a kind of meetness
To be diseas'd, ere that there was true needing.
Thus policy in love, to anticipate
The ills that were not, grew to faults assur'd,
And brought to medicine a healthful state
Which, rank of goodness, would by ill be cur'd;
  But thence I learn and find the lesson true,
  Drugs poison him that so fell sick of you.

A Riposte
Lesley Saunders

The flesh is eloquent. Incited by the mind's
incessant silent chatter, the body cries out
what stuttered words cannot – it utters facts
enacted *in flagrante*. As, a woman stuffs
her mouth with cushions lest her tongue unmuffled
revoke her rage; her anger's hungry, bitter,
her blistered lips attest her self's disgust,
there's a spider in her cup. Her lover talks
of love, but as a drug, of whose quick-drained
draught he professes her the dregs; she's slugged,
then cast aside. Though his rhetoric's passionate,
persuasive, the poet's been infected, he's caught
the sonneteer's contagion. Her unspoken oratory
upstages him, hers the truth more truly wrought.

CXIX

What potions have I drunk of Siren tears,
Distill'd from limbecks foul as hell within,
Applying fears to hopes, and hopes to fears,
Still losing when I saw myself to win!
What wretched errors hath my heart committed,
Whilst it hath thought itself so blessed never!
How have mine eyes out of their spheres been fitted,
In the distraction of this madding fever!
O benefit of ill! now I find true
That better is, by evil still made better;
And ruin'd love, when it is built anew,
Grows fairer than at first, more strong, far greater.
  So I return rebuk'd to my content,
  And gain by ill thrice more than I have spent.

Coming Back
Charlotte Amos

For ten years I have been trying to return.
From the fog of the IV drip, the drifting disconnect.
Trying to reach you. Return to your shores.

I tied myself in knots to hear the Sirens,
So they'd drown out you calling me. Drown
Thought. Thinking is for the anchored.

I am at sea.

But there is always golden light on the horizon.
Though every time I dip my oar in it, it slips away.
One day, I will bring it home to you.

I promise.

CXX

That you were once unkind befriends me now,
And for that sorrow, which I then did feel,
Needs must I under my transgression bow,
Unless my nerves were brass or hammer'd steel.
For if you were by my unkindness shaken,
As I by yours, you've pass'd a hell of time;
And I, a tyrant, have no leisure taken
To weigh how once I suffer'd in your crime.
O! that our night of woe might have remember'd
My deepest sense, how hard true sorrow hits,
And soon to you, as you to me, then tender'd
The humble salve, which wounded bosoms fits!
  But that your trespass now becomes a fee;
  Mine ransoms yours, and yours must ransom me.

Equation
Mo Jones

My fuck up + my shittiness = your fuck up + your deceit

We're quits.

CXXI

'Tis better to be vile than vile esteem'd,
When not to be receives reproach of being;
And the just pleasure lost, which is so deem'd
Not by our feeling, but by others' seeing:
For why should others' false adulterate eyes
Give salutation to my sportive blood?
Or on my frailties why are frailer spies,
Which in their wills count bad what I think good?
No, I am that I am, and they that level
At my abuses reckon up their own:
I may be straight though they themselves be bevel;
By their rank thoughts, my deeds must not be shown;
  Unless this general evil they maintain,
  All men are bad and in their badness reign.

Shit
Sadiq Malis

'Better to be wronged than to wrong',
My grandmother used to say
As she stirred rice in a pan
Larger than my head

And took whatever car, or ball,
Or catapult, my brother and I were denying
Snatching from each others
Scratching hands.

I disagreed. This was a shit proverb.
To be thought wrong in the eyes
Of the world. In your eyes.
Nothing could burn more

Dangerously. Seething with
The sense of wrong of the
Five year old who has been told
The world is fair

I pulled his hair. And denied it.

CXXII

Thy gift, thy tables, are within my brain
Full character'd with lasting memory,
Which shall above that idle rank remain,
Beyond all date; even to eternity:
Or, at the least, so long as brain and heart
Have faculty by nature to subsist;
Till each to raz'd oblivion yield his part
Of thee, thy record never can be miss'd.
That poor retention could not so much hold,
Nor need I tallies thy dear love to score;
Therefore to give them from me was I bold,
To trust those tables that receive thee more:
  To keep an adjunct to remember thee
  Were to import forgetfulness in me.

Notebook
James Miller

He gave me a moleskin
but I wrote in my head.

He gave me a camera
but I carry pictures in my heart.

He gave me a song
but I whistle on instinct.

He gave me flowers
but I could only smell their death…
plucked from the ground as a sacrifice.

CXXIII

No, Time, thou shalt not boast that I do change:
Thy pyramids built up with newer might
To me are nothing novel, nothing strange;
They are but dressings of a former sight.
Our dates are brief, and therefore we admire
What thou dost foist upon us that is old;
And rather make them born to our desire
Than think that we before have heard them told.
Thy registers and thee I both defy,
Not wondering at the present nor the past,
For thy records and what we see doth lie,
Made more or less by thy continual haste.
　This I do vow and this shall ever be;
　I will be true despite thy scythe and thee.

Someone Like You
Siobhan Harvey

And now autumn draws close, the ghost of
the woman and country you once were resurfaces
like the seasons, to haunt the lives and landscapes
you've left behind; such memories, such grief.

This is what happens to those who migrate.
Time continues unchanged as someone like you
takes first breath, watches your plane inhale the sky,
returns to the apartment you vacated, their footsteps
upon its wooden floor echoing in your heart. Mirror;

writing desk; writing paper; the bed you slept late in:
these furnish their soul as well as your own. As you
arrive on foreign soil, they write an elegy. As you
wed, they compose a sonnet. As your son is born,
their collection delivers them the Forward Prize.

This is what you miss most: your anorexia and abuse
revived by someone like you; your estranged parents
reconciled to someone like you. Nothing novel; nothing
strange. Tomorrow you'll return to the country you left,
an old street, an old house. Ajar, an old door will disclose

an old mirror holding a reflection of someone like you,
old writing paper holding the words of a poem like this
and Time's footsteps, echoes in the heart, drawing close.

CXXIV

If my dear love were but the child of state,
It might for Fortune's bastard be unfather'd,
As subject to Time's love or to Time's hate,
Weeds among weeds, or flowers with flowers gather'd.
No, it was builded far from accident;
It suffers not in smiling pomp, nor falls
Under the blow of thralled discontent,
Whereto th' inviting time our fashion calls:
It fears not policy, that heretic,
Which works on leases of short-number'd hours,
But all alone stands hugely politic,
That it nor grows with heat, nor drowns with showers.
　To this I witness call the fools of time,
　Which die for goodness, who have lived for crime.

Channel 124

Oz Hardwick

We watch the suits parading on TV,
their antiseptic voices hissing hate
while eulogising love of nation state
and uttering each new, unkind decree.
The honeyed words that drip from tongues that sting
are sickly sweet for hungry men to taste,
while common profit withers into waste
and poison pens pollute the public spring.

So, turning off the television news,
we shun the spin we will not dignify
with our attention, as we rise above
mere politics, though honest words accuse:
divested of hypocrisy, we lie
together in unregulated love.

CXXV

Were't aught to me I bore the canopy,
With my extern the outward honouring,
Or laid great bases for eternity,
Which proves more short than waste or ruining?
Have I not seen dwellers on form and favour
Lose all and more by paying too much rent
For compound sweet; forgoing simple savour,
Pitiful thrivers, in their gazing spent?
No; let me be obsequious in thy heart,
And take thou my oblation, poor but free,
Which is not mix'd with seconds, knows no art,
But mutual render, only me for thee.
  Hence, thou suborned informer! a true soul
  When most impeach'd, stands least in thy control.

Poem to Billy Shakespeare's Sonnet
Fats White

It was foggy as fuck and the water sorta reeked;
looking almost destroyed in the rough
a time travelling dog, working away in the margins
out over fields of darkness, made the clocks striking thirteen
eclipse the dama blanca and black bath salts
blacking grates on the rainbow slick oil glistening.....
the gilded Justine.
O justice this World without Dick-heads…

I'd cuddle the fuck out of you
and kiss your face endlessly right now
and do all kinds of shit till sunrise
fast-as-shit god I would…
Eat a rancid Carbuncles sandwich after blazing and it will taste
like the most delicious thing in the world.

You see
vegetarians have feelings, they feel the pain of plants.

I can hear the Perky's calling… I can hear the Xanies calling…
I been Bumping in the Trap House all night
That beat drop was so purrtty dirty
when Baby Mama walked in, I had to switch to porn
And she been counting money all morning
And you gone be rich not sleeping…
(BA-DUMP-BA)
Thank you! Thank you! I'm here all week! Try the buffet!

CXXVI

O thou, my lovely boy, who in thy power
Dost hold Time's fickle glass, his fickle hour;
Who hast by waning grown, and therein show'st
Thy lovers withering, as thy sweet self grow'st.
If Nature, sovereign mistress over wrack,
As thou goest onwards, still will pluck thee back,
She keeps thee to this purpose, that her skill
May time disgrace and wretched minutes kill.
Yet fear her, O thou minion of her pleasure!
She may detain, but not still keep, her treasure:
  Her audit (though delayed) answered must be,
  And her quietus is to render thee.

126
Rosie Johnston

My boyish love. Your solemn
tacit beauty
enchanted even Time

till in this willowed place you
chose to wane
in earth, while my heart waxes.

Your stone preserves your name,
once mine.
Chiselled dates belie vitality.

We linked hands and birled in
Nature's blessings,
Snubbed her warnings, let them swirl.

Love led us from discredit to
debit. Time
divided us in two.

I survived the severed decades
to unite here
stricken at your grave.

My heart still whirls with
precious, youthful
you.

CXXVII

In the old age black was not counted fair,
Or if it were, it bore not beauty's name;
But now is black beauty's successive heir,
And beauty slander'd with a bastard shame:
For since each hand hath put on Nature's power,
Fairing the foul with Art's false borrowed face,
Sweet beauty hath no name, no holy bower,
But is profan'd, if not lives in disgrace.
Therefore my mistress' eyes are raven black,
Her eyes so suited, and they mourners seem
At such who, not born fair, no beauty lack,
Sland'ring creation with a false esteem:
  Yet so they mourn becoming of their woe,
  That every tongue says beauty should look so.

My Face Comes In To Fashion
Nona Charles

The girl behind the Clinique counter
Is giving it the hard sell. How if I don't
Use this product, I'll be wrinkled at 40.

What's wrong with wrinkled at 40?
I think. I'll be rocking that look.
And as she daubs samples on the back

Of my hand and rubs them in with a
Circular motion, she tells me how lucky
I am. Because dark skin is in fashion.

In fashion. How could my skin be *out* of
Fashion? And she's smiling so sweetly,
And means so well, that I can't bring myself

To crush her. And I find myself wondering
Whether cats care what colour other cats are.
And whether black comes in and out of cat-fashion.

CXXVIII

How oft when thou, my music, music play'st,
Upon that blessed wood whose motion sounds
With thy sweet fingers when thou gently sway'st
The wiry concord that mine ear confounds,
Do I envy those jacks that nimble leap,
To kiss the tender inward of thy hand,
Whilst my poor lips which should that harvest reap,
At the wood's boldness by thee blushing stand!
To be so tickled, they would change their state
And situation with those dancing chips,
O'er whom thy fingers walk with gentle gait,
Making dead wood more bless'd than living lips.
  Since saucy jacks so happy are in this,
  Give them thy fingers, me thy lips to kiss.

Prokofiev's Pet
Natalya Anderson

Sergei has a new score to settle. I am powerless
against his voice, but the work affects my knees.
Madame Ulanova says 'An illusory line cannot
be drawn unless our ligaments are warmed like
bowstrings', but when Sergei mimics the tenor

saxophone I'll risk injury, limbs cold, the opus
a hot potion in my veins. For a while I left
school by different doors, crawled through
windows with broken hinges, grazed my thighs
slinking down the balcony. Sergei was there

before me, leaning under exit signs, a grin on
his face that said the evening would weaken me.
The girls in my class think we're up to no good,
morbid lovers like those crooked shadows
in the street. Sergei says their minds only play

the flute; mine plays oboes that double as French
horns. In his living room we use a pedestal as my
partner, a pillar that's heavy as a tombstone. I must
dance recklessly, with a soupçon of terror – an
ingénue about to sip her first spirit. At midnight

we drink almond tea and smoke Gitanes until
Sergei, suddenly revived, commands, 'Throw
yourself on his body; show him you yearn for
every part!' I shake out my hair, tear across
the rug. Sergei's cats leap onto the bookshelf.

CXXIX

The expense of spirit in a waste of shame
Is lust in action: and till action, lust
Is perjur'd, murderous, bloody, full of blame,
Savage, extreme, rude, cruel, not to trust;
Enjoy'd no sooner but despised straight;
Past reason hunted; and no sooner had,
Past reason hated, as a swallow'd bait,
On purpose laid to make the taker mad:
Mad in pursuit and in possession so;
Had, having, and in quest, to have extreme;
A bliss in proof, – and prov'd, a very woe;
Before, a joy propos'd; behind a dream.
  All this the world well knows; yet none knows well
  To shun the heaven that leads men to this hell.

He Will Bring Me a Rose
Valerie Darville

Tomorrow you will come and bring a rose,
while it still bears the dew upon the leaf.
To you it is a symbol of my grief,
to me a sign of other love you chose.
The ticking clock declares that time still goes,
and takes our happiness like a thief.
It is not true that life is all too brief,
but immortality on me bestows.
We did not know when first we sowed the seed,
that we would end so naked and so shorn.
The prospect at that time was glowing fair.
We did not know how soon we were to bleed.
The flower torn by sharpness of the thorn,
and joyousness replaced by heavy care.

CXXX

My mistress' eyes are nothing like the sun;
Coral is far more red, than her lips red:
If snow be white, why then her breasts are dun;
If hairs be wires, black wires grow on her head.
I have seen roses damask'd, red and white,
But no such roses see I in her cheeks;
And in some perfumes is there more delight
Than in the breath that from my mistress reeks.
I love to hear her speak, yet well I know
That music hath a far more pleasing sound:
I grant I never saw a goddess go, –
My mistress, when she walks, treads on the ground:
  And yet by heaven, I think my love as rare,
  As any she belied with false compare.

You're no Armani advert, babe
Mab Jones

You're no Armani advert, babe, less buff
than Mr Bean, with arms like bits of string
and legs like sticks. If you were a foodstuff,
you'd be something lean, a chicken wing,
perhaps, or low fat slice of beef. No man
I've ever seen was less like Hercules,
chest not like a barrel but a can –
that little one you get of processed peas
but even then bashed in and sold off cheap. Pen-
necked, pin-legged, poor-jawed, weak-cheeked. Your skinny
fingers indicate your size. Of all men
I have known you're less Mighty Mouse than Minnie,
so it was a surprise that, while you're small,
my love for you is big. Babe, you are my all.

CXXXI

Thou art as tyrannous, so as thou art,
As those whose beauties proudly make them cruel;
For well thou know'st to my dear doting heart
Thou art the fairest and most precious jewel.
Yet, in good faith, some say that thee behold,
Thy face hath not the power to make love groan;
To say they err I dare not be so bold,
Although I swear it to myself alone.
And to be sure that is not false I swear,
A thousand groans, but thinking on thy face,
One on another's neck, do witness bear
Thy black is fairest in my judgment's place.
  In nothing art thou black save in thy deeds,
  And thence this slander, as I think, proceeds.

Slander
Maylana Moohala

Loving a hack. I was never quite sure
We had the same relationship with truth.
I felt, as our moments became stories,
And you added the headline to sign off
Each encounter. And something tweeted
In my ear, that maybe you were in thrall
To the quality of your narrative.

Don't get my wrong. I'm a fan of stories.
But not all labours come in neat twelves.
Not all heroes fall. There isn't always
A beginning, a middle and an end.
You taught me that: how to make an exit
Mid paragraph. With lousy punctuation.
And no adverbs to speak of.

CXXXII

Thine eyes I love, and they, as pitying me,
Knowing thy heart torment me with disdain,
Have put on black and loving mourners be,
Looking with pretty ruth upon my pain.
And truly not the morning sun of heaven
Better becomes the grey cheeks of the east,
Nor that full star that ushers in the even,
Doth half that glory to the sober west,
As those two mourning eyes become thy face:
O! let it then as well beseem thy heart
To mourn for me since mourning doth thee grace,
And suit thy pity like in every part.
  Then will I swear beauty herself is black,
  And all they foul that thy complexion lack.

132
Loraine Saacks

Thy soul, I do perceive, writhes insecure,
Thou senses oft I've strayed around the block.
Yet conscious of the youth with which I lure,
I use thee not, as butt for me to mock.
Ne'er have I denied thee my nymph pleasures,
In truth we are but sybarites tight-tied.
Our illusions dispel any threatening measures,
While in our fantasies we both abide.
I wouldst not pain thee with the odd diversion,
I know thy flute is old, yet played in tune.
In your cocoon, I will make no incursion,
Our delusion will yet cease, but not too soon.
Thus basking in our self-deceptive sweet spell,
Wilt thy fears, my flaws and all unease dispel.

CXXXIII

Beshrew that heart that makes my heart to groan
For that deep wound it gives my friend and me!
Is't not enough to torture me alone,
But slave to slavery my sweet'st friend must be?
Me from myself thy cruel eye hath taken,
And my next self thou harder hast engross'd:
Of him, myself, and thee I am forsaken;
A torment thrice three-fold thus to be cross'd:
Prison my heart in thy steel bosom's ward,
But then my friend's heart let my poor heart bail;
Whoe'er keeps me, let my heart be his guard;
Thou canst not then use rigour in my jail:
  And yet thou wilt; for I, being pent in thee,
  Perforce am thine, and all that is in me.

Perennial Triangles
Charles Barber

To fall for one, who seems to be another's,
A human dilemma, retold throughout the ages,
In which the one that is desired, holds all cards,
Simply by the casting of a spell
Which transfixes us, two helpless victims,
Whose aims are in such diametric opposition,
To hold onto the affection and love
That one had thought secure, and contrariwise,
To tear the bond apart,
To lure the one that's pervades each waking moment,
The one that detonates such desire within my dreams,
That drives me to a torment of despair,
When seen within the orbit of that friend,
For who'm I also care, yet who I'd like
To make disappear.

If only he would do the decent thing,
Exit this far too tortuous, complex scene
The love that dares not speak, that's thwarted on my lips
Would shout from every roof top, would whisper in the ear
Of my beloved. The one that I desire
Would lie with me, not only in my dreams.

CXXXIV

So, now I have confess'd that he is thine,
And I my self am mortgag'd to thy will,
Myself I'll forfeit, so that other mine
Thou wilt restore to be my comfort still:
But thou wilt not, nor he will not be free,
For thou art covetous, and he is kind;
He learn'd but surety-like to write for me,
Under that bond that him as fast doth bind.
The statute of thy beauty thou wilt take,
Thou usurer, that putt'st forth all to use,
And sue a friend came debtor for my sake;
So him I lose through my unkind abuse.
  Him have I lost; thou hast both him and me:
  He pays the whole, and yet am I not free.

Mortgaged
Brian Deen

We'd never married. We couldn't
Afford that kind of wedding and
We'd banged tables in pubs and
Argued against that patriarchal,
Outdated institution.

Even having our three sprogs,
Our combined eyes, hair and skin
Staring back at us, somehow seemed
A thing that happened as
Naturally as wrinkles and grey flecks.

It was only now, my hand
Poised above a bit of paper
With the word 'mortgage' buried
In between three thousand
Other words I barely comprehended

That I felt a shackle. That I was
Binding myself, not to you, but
To a world where promises looked
Like contracts, and you had to use
Black ink and block capitals.

CXXXV

Whoever hath her wish, thou hast thy 'Will,'
And 'Will' to boot, and 'Will' in over-plus;
More than enough am I that vex'd thee still,
To thy sweet will making addition thus.
Wilt thou, whose will is large and spacious,
Not once vouchsafe to hide my will in thine?
Shall will in others seem right gracious,
And in my will no fair acceptance shine?
The sea, all water, yet receives rain still,
And in abundance addeth to his store;
So thou, being rich in 'Will,' add to thy 'Will'
One will of mine, to make thy large will more.
  Let no unkind 'No' fair beseechers kill;
  Think all but one, and me in that one 'Will.'

What Will you Have?
Emma Stirling

What will you have, Sir?
The beef or the chicken?

What will you have, Sir?
The marriage, three kids,
Mortgage, Christmas drinks,
Round robins, fourteen day
Holidays and cat?

What will you have, Sir?
Lazy sex on Sunday afternoons
And wild beaches where
The beer is cheap and warm
And sweat speaks?

What will you have, Sir?
A furtive grope in the cab?
Will you want tongues with that?
Will you want secrets with that?
Will you want to hold hands?
Will you want your change?
Would you like a doggy bag?
I'll get the bill. Will you want that?

CXXXVI

If thy soul check thee that I come so near,
Swear to thy blind soul that I was thy 'Will',
And will, thy soul knows, is admitted there;
Thus far for love, my love-suit, sweet, fulfil.
'Will', will fulfil the treasure of thy love,
Ay, fill it full with wills, and my will one.
In things of great receipt with ease we prove
Among a number one is reckon'd none:
Then in the number let me pass untold,
Though in thy store's account I one must be;
For nothing hold me, so it please thee hold
That nothing me, a something sweet to thee:
  Make but my name thy love, and love that still,
  And then thou lov'st me for my name is 'Will.'

Continuation - Tribute to True Unity: One Love
Jaz McKenzie

For the soul itself eternally remains
The purest form of love man's ever known.
'Will', spans the bridge where human meets divine,
Revealing the secrets time allows to flow.
The sweetest name that was, and is, is, 'Will'
For 'Will' allows pure freedom true release
Through the living branch of our divine trinity,
Until the day our human form will cease.
'Will', is the driving force behind the mind,
Taking centre-stage at every vantage point;
Pursuing integrity and love, promoting peace
When soul and will align in purest thought.
    Hence; the marriage of soul and will must always be
    Until equality and love reign, as one supreme deity.

CXXXVII

Thou blind fool, Love, what dost thou to mine eyes,
That they behold, and see not what they see?
They know what beauty is, see where it lies,
Yet what the best is take the worst to be.
If eyes, corrupt by over-partial looks,
Be anchor'd in the bay where all men ride,
Why of eyes' falsehood hast thou forged hooks,
Whereto the judgment of my heart is tied?
Why should my heart think that a several plot,
Which my heart knows the wide world's common place?
Or mine eyes, seeing this, say this is not,
To put fair truth upon so foul a face?
  In things right true my heart and eyes have err'd,
  And to this false plague are they now transferr'd.

Now and Then
Nick Eisen

It's good to see you – really –
After you left I wallowed for a while, bitter with sorrow,
but like you said from the beginning:
>We must wake up from feelings as they pass — from night to day —
>Come to bed, but keep your distance.
Fair warning –
And you were faithful to your distance, your reserve —
But I let looking at you dazzle me
even as you tried to make me see
the you beyond my dreaming gaze –
(You did, didn't you? Or is that just my feelings playing tricks?)
I broke my promise to hold back
and succumbed to my desire to possess:
- To hold on to the thrill of feeling you escape from me
even as I took you in my arms
– To find you unattainable – To think of you with others:
(You were the kind, you said, to flit from bed to bed,
through beds and distances)
– To sense the pull away in your embrace,
the glance over your shoulder for an exit,
even as you came into the room —
I asked: "Why are you like this?"
You said: "Because I choose to be."
If I'd enquired in a different way… but no.
Thinking now of what you told me then —
"We can come together – if you understand we'll come apart."
Your first words, I think, after our first kiss –
hard truth, whispered with such soft breath into my ear.

CXXXVIII

When my love swears that she is made of truth,
I do believe her though I know she lies,
That she might think me some untutor'd youth,
Unlearned in the world's false subtleties.
Thus vainly thinking that she thinks me young,
Although she knows my days are past the best,
Simply I credit her false-speaking tongue:
On both sides thus is simple truth suppressed:
But wherefore says she not she is unjust?
And wherefore say not I that I am old?
O! love's best habit is in seeming trust,
And age in love, loves not to have years told:
  Therefore I lie with her, and she with me,
  And in our faults by lies we flatter'd be.

138
Gillie Robic

I know he has no faith in my true heart
so why does he affect such nonchalance?
I love the weathered manner of his thought
yet his clamp-toothed belief is mere pretence.

He thinks I find him stale, set in his ways,
that soon I'll leave him for some callow youth
but histories outline his rumpled face
and draw me close to revel in his worth.

He is convinced I lie to him and lie
with younger men and yet he says not so,
so I cannot defend my constancy
and must pretend to what he doesn't know.

Therefore we tangle on our bed of lust;
in disarray we show each other trust.

CXXXIX

O! call not me to justify the wrong
That thy unkindness lays upon my heart;
Wound me not with thine eye, but with thy tongue:
Use power with power, and slay me not by art,
Tell me thou lov'st elsewhere; but in my sight,
Dear heart, forbear to glance thine eye aside:
What need'st thou wound with cunning, when thy might
Is more than my o'erpress'd defence can bide?
Let me excuse thee: ah! my love well knows
Her pretty looks have been mine enemies;
And therefore from my face she turns my foes,
That they elsewhere might dart their injuries:
  Yet do not so; but since I am near slain,
  Kill me outright with looks, and rid my pain.

139
Muhammad Salim

If looks could slay, you would be my killer.
True, you can expose me for who I am.
I would die, much like one in a thriller.
Your one look could prompt a gun to go BLAM!
You could make a wound in me, deep and wide.
Your unkindness can make me go insane.
If only you would be my lovely bride ...
I would not, in my heart, feel any pain.
Your pretty face makes me feel I'm ugly.
Want to be your closest companion,
But I feel that I am your enemy.
Dark clouds have gathered to blot out the sun.
Can it be that you intensely hate me?
Then kill me now, and so be rid of me.

CXL

Be wise as thou art cruel; do not press
My tongue-tied patience with too much disdain;
Lest sorrow lend me words, and words express
The manner of my pity-wanting pain.
If I might teach thee wit, better it were,
Though not to love, yet, love to tell me so; –
As testy sick men, when their deaths be near,
No news but health from their physicians know;–
For, if I should despair, I should grow mad,
And in my madness might speak ill of thee;
Now this ill-wresting world is grown so bad,
Mad slanderers by mad ears believed be.
  That I may not be so, nor thou belied,
  Bear thine eyes straight, though thy proud heart go wide.

After sonnet 140
Jo Sanders

You want me to be wise as I am cruel.
You say don't put your patience to the test,
I disrespect you, take you for a fool,
you could tell all why you are so distressed.
And now you try to give me your advice,
to say 'I love' when patently untrue.
Like ageing, addled men, at any price
believing doctors will their youth renew.
You fear that through my ways you will go mad
and in this madness might speak bad of me.
You want me to believe you would be sad
if wicked people think this true to be?
At last you seek to scare me with a threat.
Act lovingly or my true pride regret.

CXLI

In faith I do not love thee with mine eyes,
For they in thee a thousand errors note;
But 'tis my heart that loves what they despise,
Who, in despite of view, is pleased to dote.
Nor are mine ears with thy tongue's tune delighted;
Nor tender feeling, to base touches prone,
Nor taste, nor smell, desire to be invited
To any sensual feast with thee alone:
But my five wits nor my five senses can
Dissuade one foolish heart from serving thee,
Who leaves unsway'd the likeness of a man,
Thy proud heart's slave and vassal wretch to be:
  Only my plague thus far I count my gain,
  That she that makes me sin awards me pain.

"Nor do I want to abuse my delicate sense of touch by groping you"
James Trevelyan

- 'No Fear Shakespeare', Sparknotes 2016

or tell you how I really feel / nor do I want to spread cruelty / or have my future readers seek out internet scrawl for literal translations / nor do I want my work surviving in bastardised prose / or young poets responding with knowing winks / in unmetered lines / applying the thinking of their distant times to mine / nor do I ask you fumble for meaning outside your mind and this page / or frankly / expect someone your age to understand / see / you'll find it's not what they look like / how they appear first glance / it's the way they haunt your waking / sit inside you once you've turned the page / itch like a papercut / it's how the ghost of something you never thought you understood / will grapple / work you about the head / ribs / right until the day you die / then / for centuries after

CXLII

Love is my sin, and thy dear virtue hate,
Hate of my sin, grounded on sinful loving:
O! but with mine compare thou thine own state,
And thou shalt find it merits not reproving;
Or, if it do, not from those lips of thine,
That have profan'd their scarlet ornaments
And seal'd false bonds of love as oft as mine,
Robb'd others' beds' revenues of their rents.
Be it lawful I love thee, as thou lov'st those
Whom thine eyes woo as mine importune thee:
Root pity in thy heart, that, when it grows,
Thy pity may deserve to pitied be.
  If thou dost seek to have what thou dost hide,
  By self-example mayst thou be denied!

142
Anne Smith

Do you desire her, Will, for her red lips
And other qualities you don't describe?
And are you so enamoured with her hips
That you can even face her diatribe?
Or are her accusations to you true?
And do you often turn your eyes away
As often as she turns her face from you?
So did you choose her so that you could stray?
I think you did not want to settle down
So chose a lady with a roving eye
So that when she chastised you with a frown
You could remind her that she too would lie.
And yet I sense all was not quite as planned -
The more she scolds the more your passion's fanned.

CXLIII

Lo, as a careful housewife runs to catch
One of her feather'd creatures broke away,
Sets down her babe, and makes all swift dispatch
In pursuit of the thing she would have stay;
Whilst her neglected child holds her in chase,
Cries to catch her whose busy care is bent
To follow that which flies before her face,
Not prizing her poor infant's discontent;
So runn'st thou after that which flies from thee,
Whilst I thy babe chase thee afar behind;
But if thou catch thy hope, turn back to me,
And play the mother's part, kiss me, be kind;
  So will I pray that thou mayst have thy 'Will,'
  If thou turn back and my loud crying still.

The chicken and its mistress
Josephine Corcoran

My roosting place is not a house of metaphor;
My pleasures can be summarised with grain and water.
I seek sanctuary from fox and carnivore.
I cherish simple things: sunlight; absence of slaughter.
No demands from *me* about who you chase!
No clucking of the judgemental kind.
I don't pretend to know the challenges you face
In your pursuit of all you hope to find.
In relationships, and matters of the heart,
Each person, as each chicken, is unique.
Some prefer pancakes, others a custard tart
(Regarding passion, it pays not to be oblique).
Be promiscuous or chaste – I do not beg.
Throw me corn. I will honour you with an egg.

CXLIV

Two loves I have of comfort and despair,
Which like two spirits do suggest me still:
The better angel is a man right fair,
The worser spirit a woman colour'd ill.
To win me soon to hell, my female evil,
Tempteth my better angel from my side,
And would corrupt my saint to be a devil,
Wooing his purity with her foul pride.
And whether that my angel be turn'd fiend,
Suspect I may, yet not directly tell;
But being both from me, both to each friend,
I guess one angel in another's hell:
  Yet this shall I ne'er know, but live in doubt,
  Till my bad angel fire my good one out.

Fragment from William Shakespeare'e diary, recently discovered
Arthur Fox

It's unbelievable
That she's gone off with him, my darling boy
They are together now , indulging fulsomely
With I know not what of earthly pleasures.
I know not how I shall survive this day.
He was my lovely friend, she was my dearest treasure.
What will Ben Jonson do if he finds out?
I know. He'll write a play that sends me up
'The playwright Out Of His Humour'
Or some such thing, the cur.
I'll throw him in the Thames if he should dare
Turn me into the double cuckold
Laughing stock of London. I'm the man
Not him and he wont care how deeply I've been hurt.
Well to hell with it. I'll leave those two to sweat
And no more from me will either of them get
Of all the gifts I've lavished on them in the past.
And as for Ben, I'll show him, beat him to it
Write a play. But what though? The Whore Of Babylon?
No that's been done. Delilah? Salome? Best not.
It shall be a history
Of Cleopatra and her Antony. How he betrays his wife
To go with her, and how she in turn does much the same to him.
A story of lascivious lust and honour and betrayal of trust.
A must when it is done for every Londoner to see.
And so enough of all my mental strife.
I shall return to Stratford, write my play,
And seek out my adoring wife.

CXLV

Those lips that Love's own hand did make,
Breathed forth the sound that said 'I hate',
To me that languish'd for her sake:
But when she saw my woeful state,
Straight in her heart did mercy come,
Chiding that tongue that ever sweet
Was us'd in giving gentle doom;
And taught it thus anew to greet;
'I hate' she alter'd with an end,
That followed it as gentle day,
Doth follow night, who like a fiend
From heaven to hell is flown away.
  'I hate', from hate away she threw,
  And sav'd my life, saying 'not you'.

'T' word
Debby Grayson

You used the 'T' word:
"We need to talk."
From your Adonis lips that hateful phrase
flew like an arrow through the waves,
pierced my frozen ear.

Certain you'd hear my gasping heart,
I cast the curséd phone.
Like the hunted, my love grew ill.
"We need to talk."
Who'd have thought those words could kill?

Through fitful night the heavens roared:
Would the slaughter be gentle
or swift as a sword?
But all endings are the same –
"We need to talk"
is never sweet by any name.

And then you came
and bared the Truth:
That love is lasting, but not youth.
My soul was spared
by your startling request!

You used the 'M' word –
I said "Yes"!

CXLVI

Poor soul, the centre of my sinful earth,
My sinful earth these rebel powers array,
Why dost thou pine within and suffer dearth,
Painting thy outward walls so costly gay?
Why so large cost, having so short a lease,
Dost thou upon thy fading mansion spend?
Shall worms, inheritors of this excess,
Eat up thy charge? Is this thy body's end?
Then soul, live thou upon thy servant's loss,
And let that pine to aggravate thy store;
Buy terms divine in selling hours of dross;
Within be fed, without be rich no more:
  So shall thou feed on Death, that feeds on men,
  And Death once dead, there's no more dying then.

The body and the soul
Charley Alldridge

There's no more dying then –
    that's what you said –
and the words echo
      and resound
with a promise they can't keep.

The immortality you found
    was rooted in your soul,
        perhaps,
  if such things are real...
but the words that live,
    were delivered in ink –
  not free-floating thought –
    by the very instrument
your arguments dismiss.

The body and soul
are the lock and key –
co-dependent,
each meaningless alone...
therefore, concede your harsh conceit.

CXLVII

My love is as a fever longing still,
For that which longer nurseth the disease;
Feeding on that which doth preserve the ill,
The uncertain sickly appetite to please.
My reason, the physician to my love,
Angry that his prescriptions are not kept,
Hath left me, and I desperate now approve
Desire is death, which physic did except.
Past cure I am, now Reason is past care,
And frantic-mad with evermore unrest;
My thoughts and my discourse as madmen's are,
At random from the truth vainly express'd;
  For I have sworn thee fair, and thought thee bright,
  Who art as black as hell, as dark as night.

The Bug
Tessa Foley

My son, my boy, my shiftless, lights-off pride and joy,
You say this is a sickness, heart disease
And lie upstairs, the sixth form calls just once or twice
And lets you lie, but this is not an ill, this is a
Brush with cruellish gruel, A girl or boy with angles
All about them, their breath still festers in your ear
They will remain a weevil crawling in your soup
And stop my child from eating tea.

Your idol elsewhere smiles like xylophone and you stay home
And curled as pupa in the rut that stinks and I can't clean,
I knock for your attention, but you are window-guarding
With a paper face, I don't mention the phone, really,
Never rang, you're on your own, enjoying pine of bedstead
And of longing. You'd never say with smoked remains
All curling in your gut, but I'm to guess and be too
Old to understand.

But once with clammy cheeks and gunshot breath,
I'd had the same. Before your father took the sting away,
The one before, the only one - a glory cactus on a peak
So high I couldnt gasp, An opiate that snatched himself away,
A weedy, premature obsession, dying in its early birth.
Your dad he fluffed the pillows and now the wire was earth,
So just because I'm sat on sofas dumbly facing forward and sickness?
Can't attack, I know your nasusea, Son: Now find a boring suitor.

CXLVIII

O me! what eyes hath Love put in my head,
Which have no correspondence with true sight;
Or, if they have, where is my judgment fled,
That censures falsely what they see aright?
If that be fair whereon my false eyes dote,
What means the world to say it is not so?
If it be not, then love doth well denote
Love's eye is not so true as all men's: no,
How can it? O! how can Love's eye be true,
That is so vexed with watching and with tears?
No marvel then, though I mistake my view;
The sun itself sees not, till heaven clears.
  O cunning Love! with tears thou keep'st me blind,
  Lest eyes well-seeing thy foul faults should find.

"What use is the eye to the one who loves?"
Isobel Dixon

What Use is the eye to the one who loves?
May as well stumble blindfold from the first,
knowing how keenly light and shape deceive
when the heart is gripped, how much what's wished
is what's perceived. The line of a wrist, his crisp,
white sleeve – whole cities have fallen for less
than this. And wandering, lost, in ardour's mist,
you miss the vital signs: that sigh, curled lip,
how ready suddenly he is to up and leave.
But that's to come. This rumpled sheet
flags your surrender, you breathe the cleaving
essences – for now, love, ignorance is bliss.
The steady gaze you once believed you had
is just a fallacy. You close your eyes to kiss.

CXLIX

Canst thou, O cruel! say I love thee not,
When I against myself with thee partake?
Do I not think on thee, when I forgot
Am of my self, all tyrant, for thy sake?
Who hateth thee that I do call my friend,
On whom frown'st thou that I do fawn upon,
Nay, if thou lour'st on me, do I not spend
Revenge upon myself with present moan?
What merit do I in my self respect,
That is so proud thy service to despise,
When all my best doth worship thy defect,
Commanded by the motion of thine eyes?
  But, love, hate on, for now I know thy mind;
  Those that can see thou lov'st, and I am blind.

I might prefer Wordsworth
Nick Alldridge

So let me see - these questions deserve
a thoughtful and sincere reply:
well first your lack of reserve
is as manly as a butterfly.
And I know your thoughts are for your art,
so turning up here with fourteen lines
is never even going to start
to make amends for all those times
you spent with your mates, getting pissed.
And as for my enemies I know full well
I can't rely on you to stand firm amidst
a host of yellow daffodils.
And when you whine at everything
it's hard to spot where one sob stops
and the next one starts to wring
itself out in nonstop soppy drops.
So please, if you would win my heart,
could you play a little hard to get?
I know you are a desperate fart
but could you show some self-respect?
So no, my love, for now I hope
you'll come to know my mind
is not satisfied by a fool who mopes.
The point in being irresistible, you'll find,
is not to seek out boggy ground,
where no resistance can be found.

CL

O! from what power hast thou this powerful might,
With insufficiency my heart to sway?
To make me give the lie to my true sight,
And swear that brightness doth not grace the day?
Whence hast thou this becoming of things ill,
That in the very refuse of thy deeds
There is such strength and warrantise of skill,
That, in my mind, thy worst all best exceeds?
Who taught thee how to make me love thee more,
The more I hear and see just cause of hate?
O! though I love what others do abhor,
With others thou shouldst not abhor my state:
  If thy unworthiness rais'd love in me,
  More worthy I to be belov'd of thee.

'In my mind, thy worst all best exceeds'
Suzannah Evans

At our worst we sleep with our backs curled
against each other, two angry prawns.
Our bed is a boat lost on the sea
of the wet weekend. At our worst

we are each others' needy dogs
and we bite our nails down into our fingers.
You say *I'm sad* and I say *I'm sad too*
we take our separate pills.

Today you judged every person too harshly
and I swore loudly at the TV news.
Your hand finds mine under the bedclothes
and I hold it like a charm until morning.

CLI

Love is too young to know what conscience is,
Yet who knows not conscience is born of love?
Then, gentle cheater, urge not my amiss,
Lest guilty of my faults thy sweet self prove:
For, thou betraying me, I do betray
My nobler part to my gross body's treason;
My soul doth tell my body that he may
Triumph in love; flesh stays no farther reason,
But rising at thy name doth point out thee,
As his triumphant prize. Proud of this pride,
He is contented thy poor drudge to be,
To stand in thy affairs, fall by thy side.
  No want of conscience hold it that I call
  Her 'love,' for whose dear love I rise and fall.

151
Barney Norris

She's chucked him for a younger man.
He's wanking in a hotel room
like Philip Larkin, on his own
and leaving poems tossed across the sheets.

CLII

In loving thee thou know'st I am forsworn,
But thou art twice forsworn, to me love swearing;
In act thy bed-vow broke, and new faith torn,
In vowing new hate after new love bearing:
But why of two oaths' breach do I accuse thee,
When I break twenty? I am perjur'd most;
For all my vows are oaths but to misuse thee,
And all my honest faith in thee is lost:
For I have sworn deep oaths of thy deep kindness,
Oaths of thy love, thy truth, thy constancy;
And, to enlighten thee, gave eyes to blindness,
Or made them swear against the thing they see;
  For I have sworn thee fair; more perjur'd I,
  To swear against the truth so foul a lie!

The Guilty
John Challis

For months I strove to prove your indiscretion.
Everything that came close to fitting fit my theory.
My case was watertight for presentation to the jury.
Imagine this: your bf/gf hands over a dossier
of photographs and emails, carefully chosen evidence.
What does it say? *The guilty seek their punishment.*

I've always thought it bull in films when lovers let
the other go because they pine for someone else.
Secretly the noble one must have something on the side.
No one wants to be alone. In life we wrestle
with our minds, do little else for days. In the end

I took the passive road, for years unread the file,
but knew how, by imagining, I admitted that the proof
I'd found pointed only to the affair I was to have.

CLIII

Cupid laid by his brand and fell asleep:
A maid of Dian's this advantage found,
And his love-kindling fire did quickly steep
In a cold valley-fountain of that ground;
Which borrow'd from this holy fire of Love,
A dateless lively heat, still to endure,
And grew a seeting bath, which yet men prove
Against strange maladies a sovereign cure.
But at my mistress' eye Love's brand new-fired,
The boy for trial needs would touch my breast;
I, sick withal, the help of bath desired,
And thither hied, a sad distemper'd guest,
  But found no cure, the bath for my help lies
  Where Cupid got new fire; my mistress' eyes.

Found No Cure
Rosamund Taylor

You don't quench my fire, love, never,
it may burn down to embers but still glows
and rises new, brash, gaudy: whenever
I see you, your throat, navel, knobbly toes,
I'm awake, aching to hear your low sighs,
shivering as you shiver. I'm wet and bright.

I've licked shy mouths, kissed other thighs,
leant my shins on different backs on nights
spent staring at damp ceilings – but it's you
I kneel for over and over. I sleep best
smelling you on my chin, my lips. I never knew
that in your body's folds I'd find such rest –
here my fire gutters, may sometimes falter,
but is renewed, like a candle on an altar.

CLIV

The little Love-god lying once asleep,
Laid by his side his heart-inflaming brand,
Whilst many nymphs that vow'd chaste life to keep
Came tripping by; but in her maiden hand
The fairest votary took up that fire
Which many legions of true hearts had warm'd;
And so the general of hot desire
Was, sleeping, by a virgin hand disarm'd.
This brand she quenched in a cool well by,
Which from Love's fire took heat perpetual,
Growing a bath and healthful remedy,
For men diseas'd; but I, my mistress' thrall,
  Came there for cure and this by that I prove,
  Love's fire heats water, water cools not love.

The Secret Pools
Emma Simon

Mine is unmirrored. Water flecked with silt,
a sludgy glitter; depths obscured by weed.
Bone-steeping cold. Screened from city life
by oak and birch, drawn like heavy curtains
in high summer, trapping thick air. The nymphs
- grey hair tucked into bathing caps - strike out
a bracing crawl, eye-ball the rampant ducks
who prink and snap like wind-stuck demigods.
Bathers, at ease with form, with flesh, with hair,
laugh with their mates, dip beneath the surface
of late afternoons. The nymphs sing to the woman
on the landing stage, psyching herself
to dive: *Come in, come in, the water's fine.*
It won't cool love, so why not drown in it?

LIVE CANON